CONTENTS

CHOCOLATE 101

You could search the world over and never find a confection more beloved than chocolate! Whether you're in the mood for crunchy cookies, gooey brownies or decadent cheesecake, this Chocolate Lover's Collection will fulfill your chocolate fantasy.

TYPES OF CHOCOLATE

Pure chocolate is made up of cocoa solids and cocoa butter. The different varieties of chocolate are created just by adding or subtracting ingredients. Here are the most common types.

Unsweetened Chocolate

Also called bitter or baking chocolate, this is pure chocolate with no sugar or flavorings added. It is used in baking and is packaged in individually wrapped 1-ounce squares.

Bittersweet Chocolate

Bittersweet chocolate is pure chocolate with some sugar added. It is available in 1-ounce squares or in bars.

Semisweet Chocolate

Semisweet chocolate is pure chocolate combined with sugar and extra cocoa butter. It is sold in a variety of forms, including 1-ounce squares, bars, chips and chunks.

Milk Chocolate

Milk chocolate is pure chocolate with sugar, extra cocoa butter and milk solids added. It is available in various shapes—bars, chips, stars, etc.

White Chocolate

White chocolate is white because it contains no cocoa solids. It is made up of cocoa butter, milk solids and vanilla and is available in chips and bars.

Unsweetened Cocoa

This is formed by extracting most of the cocoa butter from pure chocolate and grinding the remaining chocolate solids into a powder. Since most of the cocoa butter is removed, it is low in fat.

MELTING CHOCOLATE

Make sure the utensils used for melting are completely dry. Moisture causes the chocolate to "seize," which means that it becomes stiff and grainy. If this happens, add ½ teaspoon shortening (not butter) for each ounce of chocolate and stir until smooth. Chocolate scorches easily, and once scorched it cannot be used. Follow one of these three methods for successful melting.

Double Boiler

Place the chocolate in the top of a double boiler or in a heatproof bowl over hot, not boiling, water; stir chocolate until smooth. (Make sure that the water remains just below a simmer and is one inch below the bottom of the top pan.) Be careful that no steam or water gets into the chocolate.

EASY EASEL RECIPES

INDEX

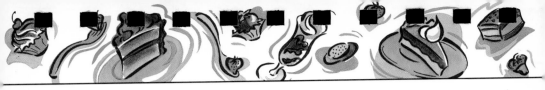

Direct Heat

Place the chocolate in a heavy saucepan and melt over very low heat, stirring constantly. Remove the chocolate from heat as soon as it is melted. Be sure to watch the chocolate carefully because it is easily scorched when using this method.

Microwave Oven

Place an unwrapped 1-ounce square or 1 cup of chips in a small microwavable bowl. Microwave on HIGH 1 to 1½ minutes, stirring after 1 minute. Stir the chocolate at 30-second intervals until smooth. Be sure to stir microwaved chocolate since it may retain its original shape even when melted.

STORING INFORMATION

Chocolate

Since both heat and moisture adversely affect chocolate, it should be stored at room temperature wrapped in foil or waxed paper. Unsweetened, bittersweet and semisweet chocolate can be stored a very long time, as long as 10 years. Because they contain milk solids, white chocolate and milk chocolate have a much shorter shelf life, about 9 months.

Cookies, Bar Cookies and Brownies

Unbaked cookie dough can be refrigerated for up to 1 week or frozen for up to 6 weeks.

Rolls of dough should be sealed tightly in plastic wrap; other doughs should be stored in airtight containers. For convenience, label dough or container with baking information.

Store soft and crisp cookies separately at room temperature to prevent changes in texture and flavor. Keep soft cookies in airtight containers. If they begin to dry out, add a piece of apple or bread to the container to help them retain moisture. Store crisp cookies in containers with loose-fitting lids to prevent moisture buildup.

EASY EASEL
RECIPES

CHOCOLATE CHIP COOKIE DOUGH FUDGE

⅓ cup butter, melted
⅓ cup packed brown sugar
¾ cup all-purpose flour
½ teaspoon salt, divided
1⅓ cups mini semisweet chocolate chips, divided
1 package (1 pound) powdered sugar
1 package (8 ounces) cream cheese, softened
1 teaspoon vanilla

1. Line 8- or 9-inch square pan with foil, leaving 1-inch overhang on sides. Lightly butter foil.

2. Combine butter and brown sugar in small bowl. Stir in flour and ¼ teaspoon salt. Stir in ⅓ cup chips. Form dough into a ball. Place on plastic wrap; flatten into a disc. Wrap disc in plastic wrap; freeze 10 minutes or until firm.

3. Unwrap dough; cut into ½-inch pieces; refrigerate.

4. Place powdered sugar, cream cheese, vanilla and remaining ¼ teaspoon salt in large bowl. Beat with electric mixer at low speed until combined. Beat at medium speed until smooth.

5. Melt remaining 1 cup chips in small saucepan over low heat, stirring constantly.

6. Add to cream cheese mixture; beat just until blended. Stir in chilled cookie dough pieces. Spread evenly in prepared pan.

7. Refrigerate until firm. Remove from pan by lifting fudge and foil using foil handles. Cut into squares.

Makes about 3 to 4 dozen candies

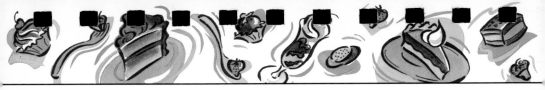

Store cookies with sticky glazes, fragile decorations and icings in single layers between sheets of waxed paper. Bar cookies and brownies may be stored in their own baking pan. Cover with foil or plastic wrap when cooled. Freeze baked cookies in airtight containers or freezer bags for up to 6 months. Thaw cookies and brownies unwrapped at room temperature. Meringue-based cookies do not freeze well and chocolate-dipped cookies may discolor if frozen.

Cakes and Cheesecakes

Store one-layer cakes in their baking pans, tightly covered. Store two- or three-layer cakes in a cake-saver. If the cake has a fluffy or cooked frosting, insert a teaspoon handle under the edge of the cover to prevent an airtight seal and moisture buildup. Cheesecakes and cakes with whipped cream frosting or cream fillings should be stored in the refrigerator for up to 1 week.

Unfrosted cakes can be frozen for up to 4 months if well wrapped in plastic. Thaw in their wrapping at room temperature. Frosted cakes should be frozen unwrapped until the frosting hardens, and then wrapped and sealed; freeze for up to 2 months. To thaw, remove the wrapping and thaw at room temperature or in the refrigerator. Cheesecakes and cakes with fruit or custard fillings do not freeze well, as they become soggy when thawed.

Candy

Store candy between sheets of waxed paper or plastic wrap in an airtight container in a cool, dry place. Store hard candies and soft candies separately to prevent changes in texture and flavor. When candy is stored properly, it will keep up to 2 to 3 weeks. Candies like fudge and caramels can be wrapped airtight and frozen for up to 1 year. Thaw candy unwrapped at room temperature for 3 hours.

CASHEW MACADAMIA CRUNCH

2 cups (11.5 ounce package) HERSHEY'S Milk Chocolate Chips
¾ cup coarsely chopped salted or unsalted cashews
¾ cup coarsely chopped salted or unsalted macadamia nuts
½ cup (1 stick) butter, softened
½ cup sugar
2 tablespoons light corn syrup

1. Line 9-inch square pan with foil, extending foil over edges of pan. Butter foil. Cover bottom of prepared pan with chocolate chips.

2. Combine cashews, macadamia nuts, butter, sugar and corn syrup in large heavy skillet; cook over low heat, stirring constantly, until butter is melted and sugar is dissolved. Increase heat to medium; cook, stirring constantly, until mixture begins to cling together and turns golden brown.

3. Pour mixture over chocolate chips in pan, spreading evenly. Cool. Refrigerate until chocolate is firm. Remove from pan; peel off foil. Break into pieces. Store, tightly covered in cool, dry place. *Makes about 1½ pounds*

Classic Chippers

Chocolate Crackletops (page 17)

TRIPLE LAYER CHOCOLATE MINTS

6 ounces semisweet chocolate, chopped
6 ounces white chocolate, chopped
1 teaspoon peppermint extract
6 ounces milk chocolate, chopped

1. Line 8-inch square pan with foil, leaving 1-inch overhang on sides.

2. Place semisweet chocolate in top of double boiler over simmering water. Stir until melted. Remove from heat.

3. Spread melted chocolate onto bottom of prepared pan. Let stand until firm. (If not firm after 45 minutes, refrigerate 10 minutes.)

4. Melt white chocolate in clean double boiler; stir in peppermint extract. Spread over semisweet chocolate layer. Shake pan to spread evenly. Let stand 45 minutes or until set.

5. Melt milk chocolate in same double boiler. Spread over white chocolate layer. Shake pan to spread evenly. Let stand 45 minutes or until set.

6. Cut mints into 16 (2-inch) squares. Remove from pan by lifting mints and foil with foil handles.

7. Cut each square diagonally into 2 triangles. Cut in half again to make 64 small triangles.   *Makes 64 mints*

ORIGINAL NESTLÉ® TOLL HOUSE®
CHOCOLATE CHIP COOKIES

2¼ cups all-purpose flour
1 teaspoon baking soda
1 teaspoon salt
1 cup (2 sticks) butter, softened
¾ cup granulated sugar
¾ cup packed brown sugar
1 teaspoon vanilla extract
2 eggs
2 cups (12-ounce package) NESTLÉ®
   TOLL HOUSE® Semi-Sweet Chocolate
   Morsels
1 cup chopped nuts

COMBINE flour, baking soda and salt in small bowl. Beat butter, granulated sugar, brown sugar and vanilla in large mixer bowl. Add eggs, one at a time, beating well after each addition.

Gradually beat in flour mixture. Stir in morsels and nuts. Drop by rounded tablespoon onto ungreased baking sheets.

BAKE in preheated 375°F. oven for 9 to 11 minutes or until golden brown. Cool on baking sheets for 2 minutes; remove to wire racks to cool completely.

Makes about 5 dozen cookies

COOKIES AND CREAM CHEESECAKE BONBONS

24 chocolate cream-filled cookies, divided
1 package (8 ounces) cream cheese, softened
1 cup nonfat dry milk
1 teaspoon vanilla
1 package (1 pound) powdered sugar

1. Coarsely chop 12 cookies; set aside.

2. Place remaining 12 cookies in food processor; process until fine crumbs form. Place crumbs on baking sheet lined with waxed paper; set aside.

3. Beat cream cheese, dry milk and vanilla in medium bowl with electric mixer at medium speed until smooth. Beat in powdered sugar, 1 cup at a time, at low speed until mixture is smooth.

Stir in reserved chopped cookies. Refrigerate 2 hours or until firm.

4. Shape rounded tablespoonfuls cream cheese mixture into balls. Roll balls in reserved cookie crumbs.

Makes about 3 dozen bonbons

CHOCOLATE CHIP 'N OATMEAL COOKIES

1 package (18.25 or 18.5 ounces) yellow cake mix
1 cup quick-cooking rolled oats, uncooked
¾ cup butter or margarine, softened
2 eggs
1 cup HERSHEY'S Semi-Sweet Chocolate Chips

Preheat oven to 350°F. In large bowl, combine cake mix, oats, butter and eggs; mix well. Stir in chocolate chips. Drop by rounded teaspoonfuls onto ungreased cookie sheets.

Bake 10 to 12 minutes or until very lightly browned. Cool slightly; remove from cookie sheets to wire racks. Cool completely.

Makes about 4 dozen cookies

Cook's Notes:

To get the number of cookies listed in a drop cookie recipe, drop cookie dough with a tableware spoon, not a measuring spoon.

EASY EASEL RECIPES

EASY TURTLE FUDGE

1 package (12 ounces) semisweet
  chocolate chips
2 ounces bittersweet chocolate, chopped
1 cup sweetened condensed milk
¼ teaspoon salt
30 individually wrapped caramel candies,
  unwrapped
1 tablespoon water
40 pecan halves

1. Grease 11×7-inch pan; set aside.

2. Melt chips in medium saucepan over low heat, stirring constantly. Stir in bittersweet chocolate until melted. Stir in sweetened condensed milk and salt until smooth. Spread evenly in prepared pan; cover with foil. Refrigerate until firm.

3. Cut fudge into 40 squares. Transfer to baking sheet lined with waxed paper, placing squares ½ inch apart.

4. Place caramels and water in small saucepan. Heat over low heat until melted, stirring frequently. Drizzle fudge pieces with caramel mixture. Top each piece with 1 pecan half. *Makes 40 candies*

CHOCOLATE CHIP SHORTBREAD

½ **cup butter, softened**
½ **cup sugar**
1 **teaspoon vanilla**
1 **cup all-purpose flour**
¼ **teaspoon salt**
½ **cup mini semisweet chocolate chips**

Preheat oven to 375°F. Beat butter and sugar in large bowl with electric mixer at medium speed until fluffy. Beat in vanilla. Add flour and salt; beat at low speed. Stir in chips.

Divide dough in half. Press each half into ungreased 8-inch round cake pan.

Bake 12 minutes or until edges are golden brown. Score shortbread with sharp knife, taking care not to cut completely through shortbread. Make 8 wedges per pan.

Let pans stand on wire racks 10 minutes. Invert shortbread onto wire racks; cool completely. Break into triangles.

Makes 16 cookies

Cook's Notes:
Butter can be stored in the refrigerator up to 1 month. Be sure to wrap it airtight, as butter readily absorbs flavors and odors from other items in the refrigerator.

LAYERED TOASTED HAZELNUT FUDGE

1½ cups chopped hazelnuts, divided
2 cups granulated sugar
1 cup packed brown sugar
1 can (5 ounces) evaporated milk
½ cup butter
1 jar (7 ounces) marshmallow creme
1½ teaspoons vanilla
½ teaspoon salt
6 ounces semisweet chocolate, chopped

Preheat oven to 350°F. Line 8-inch square pan with foil, leaving 1-inch overhang on sides. Lightly butter foil.

Place 1 cup hazelnuts in food processor. Process until a smooth peanut butter consistency is reached; set aside.

Combine sugars, evaporated milk and butter in large saucepan; bring to a boil over medium heat, stirring frequently.

Attach candy thermometer to side of pan making sure bulb is submerged in sugar mixture but not touching bottom of pan.

Continue boiling 5 minutes or until sugar mixture reaches soft-ball stage (238°F) on candy thermometer, stirring constantly. Reduce heat to low; stir in marshmallow creme, vanilla and salt until blended. Remove from heat.

Transfer 2 cups sugar mixture to medium bowl; stir in reserved hazelnut paste. Add chocolate to sugar mixture in saucepan; stir until blended. Stir in remaining chopped hazelnuts.

Pour chocolate mixture into prepared pan; spread evenly. Pour reserved hazelnut mixture on top of chocolate mixture; spread evenly.

Score into 36 squares while fudge is still warm. Cool completely. Remove from pan by lifting fudge and foil using foil handles. Cut into squares.   *Makes 3 dozen candies*

CHOCOLATE CHIP MACAROONS

2½ cups flaked coconut
⅔ cup mini semisweet chocolate chips
⅔ cup sweetened condensed milk
1 teaspoon vanilla

1. Preheat oven to 350°F. Grease cookie sheets.

2. Combine coconut, chocolate chips, milk and vanilla in medium bowl; mix until well blended.

3. Drop dough by rounded teaspoonfuls 2 inches apart onto greased cookie sheets. Press dough gently with back of spoon to flatten slightly.

4. Bake 10 to 12 minutes or until light golden brown. Let cookies stand on cookie sheets 1 minute.

5. Remove cookies to wire racks; cool completely.   *Makes about 3½ dozen cookies*

Cook's Notes:

Store unopened cans of sweetened condensed milk at room temperature up to 6 months. Store any leftover milk in an airtight container up to 5 days.

FUDGY BANANA ROCKY ROAD CLUSTERS

**1 package (12 ounces) semisweet
  chocolate chips (2 cups)**
⅓ cup peanut butter
3 cups miniature marshmallows
1 cup unsalted peanuts
1 cup banana chips

Place chocolate chips and peanut butter in
large microwaveable bowl. Microwave at
HIGH 2 minutes or until chips are melted
and mixture is smooth,
stirring twice.

Fold in marshmallows,
peanuts and banana
chips.

Line baking sheets with
waxed paper. Grease
waxed paper.

Drop rounded tablespoonfuls candy mixture
onto prepared baking sheets; refrigerate until
firm. Store in airtight container in
refrigerator.   *Makes 2½ to 3 dozen clusters*

....

Cook's Notes:
***Full of flavor and crunch, this gooey treat is one
the kids will love to help you make!***

....

CHOCOLATE CHIP ALMOND BISCOTTI

2¾ cups all-purpose flour
1½ teaspoons baking powder
¼ teaspoon salt
½ cup butter, softened
1 cup sugar
3 eggs
3 tablespoons amaretto (almond-flavored liqueur)
1 tablespoon water
1 cup mini semisweet chocolate chips
1 cup sliced almonds, toasted and coarsely chopped

Combine flour, baking powder and salt in medium bowl. Beat butter and sugar in large bowl with electric mixer at medium speed until light and fluffy. Beat in eggs, 1 at a time, beating well after each addition. Add liqueur and water. Gradually add flour mixture. Stir in chips and almonds.

Divide dough into fourths. Spread each quarter evenly down center of a sheet of waxed paper. Using waxed paper to hold dough, roll it back and forth to form a 15-inch log. Wrap securely. Refrigerate about 2 hours or until firm.

Preheat oven to 375°F. Lightly grease cookie sheets. Place each log on prepared cookie sheets. With floured hands, shape each log 2 inches wide and ½ inch thick.

Bake 15 minutes. Remove from oven. Cut each log with serrated knife into 1-inch diagonal slices. Return slices, cut side up, to cookie sheets; bake 7 minutes. Turn cookies over; bake 7 minutes or until cut surfaces are golden brown and cookies are dry. Cool completely on wire racks.

Makes about 4 dozen cookies

DOUBLE CHOCOLATE TRUFFLES

½ cup whipping cream
1 tablespoon butter or margarine
4 bars (1 ounce each) HERSHEY'S Semi-Sweet Baking Chocolate, broken into pieces
1 HERSHEY'S Milk Chocolate Bar (7 ounces), broken into pieces
1 tablespoon amaretto (almond-flavored liqueur) *or* ¼ to ½ teaspoon almond extract
Ground almonds

In small saucepan, combine whipping cream and butter. Cook over medium heat, stirring constantly, just until mixture is very hot. Do not boil. Remove from heat; add chocolate, chocolate bar pieces and liqueur. Stir with whisk until smooth. Press plastic

wrap directly onto surface; cool several hours or until mixture is firm enough to handle. Shape into 1-inch balls; roll in almonds to coat. Refrigerate until firm, about 2 hours. Store in tightly covered container in refrigerator.   *Makes about 2 dozen candies*

COWBOY COOKIES

½ **cup butter, softened**
½ **cup packed light brown sugar**
¼ **cup granulated sugar**
1 **egg**
1 **teaspoon vanilla**
1 **cup all-purpose flour**
2 **tablespoons unsweetened cocoa**
    powder
½ **teaspoon baking powder**
¼ **teaspoon baking soda**
1 **cup uncooked rolled oats**
1 **cup (6 ounces)**
    semisweet
    chocolate chips
½ **cup raisins**
½ **cup chopped nuts**

Preheat oven to 375°F.
Lightly grease cookie
sheets or line with
parchment paper.

Beat butter with sugars in
large bowl until blended.

Add egg and vanilla; beat until fluffy.
Combine flour, cocoa, baking powder and
baking soda in small bowl; stir into butter
mixture. Add oats, chocolate chips, raisins
and nuts. Drop by rounded teaspoonfuls 2
inches apart onto prepared cookie sheets.

Bake 10 to 12 minutes or until lightly
browned around edges. Remove to wire racks
to cool. *Makes about 4 dozen cookies*

GERMAN CHOCOLATE NO-COOK FUDGE

3 (4-ounce) packages German's sweet chocolate, broken into pieces
1 cup (6 ounces) semisweet chocolate chips
1 can (14 ounces) sweetened condensed milk
1 cup chopped pecans
2 teaspoons vanilla
36 pecan halves (optional)

Butter 8-inch square pan; set aside. Melt chocolate and chips in small saucepan over very low heat, stirring constantly. Remove from heat. Stir in condensed milk, chopped pecans and vanilla until combined. Spread in prepared pan. Arrange pecan halves on fudge. Score fudge into squares with knife. Refrigerate until firm.

Cut into squares. Store in refrigerator. Bring to room temperature before serving.

Makes about 2 pounds

Cook's Notes:

Pecans can be stored in an airtight container up to 3 months in the refrigerator or up to 6 months in the freezer.

DOUBLE CHOCOLATE CHUNK COOKIES

4 squares BAKER'S® Semi-Sweet Chocolate, divided
½ cup (1 stick) margarine or butter, slightly softened
½ cup granulated sugar
¼ cup firmly packed brown sugar
1 egg
1 teaspoon vanilla
1 cup all-purpose flour
½ teaspoon CALUMET® Baking Powder
¼ teaspoon salt
¾ cup chopped walnuts (optional)
4 squares BAKER'S® Semi-Sweet Chocolate

MELT 1 square chocolate; set aside. Cut 3 squares chocolate into large (½-inch) chunks; set aside.

BEAT margarine, sugars, egg and vanilla until light and fluffy. Stir in 1 square melted chocolate. Mix in flour, baking powder and salt. Stir in chocolate chunks and walnuts. Refrigerate 30 minutes.

HEAT oven to 375°F. Drop dough by heaping tablespoonfuls, about 2 inches apart, onto greased cookie sheets. Bake for 8 minutes or until lightly browned. Cool 5 minutes on cookie sheets. Remove and finish cooling on wire racks.

MELT 4 squares chocolate. Dip ½ of each cookie into melted chocolate. Let stand on waxed paper until chocolate is firm.
Makes about 2 dozen cookies

EASY EASEL RECIPES

CHERRY WALNUT WHITE CHOCOLATE FUDGE

3 cups sugar
1 cup whipping cream
½ cup butter
¼ cup light corn syrup
8 ounces premium white chocolate, chopped
1 teaspoon vanilla
1 cup chopped dried cherries
1 cup toasted walnuts, chopped

Spray 9×9-inch pan with nonstick cooking spray. Set aside.

Combine sugar, cream, butter and syrup in large saucepan. Cook over medium heat until sugar dissolves and mixture comes to a boil, stirring frequently.

Attach candy thermometer to side of pan, making sure bulb is submerged in sugar mixture but not touching bottom of pan. Continue cooking about 6 minutes or until sugar mixture reaches soft-ball stage (234°F) on thermometer, stirring frequently.

Remove from heat; let stand 10 minutes. (Do not stir.) Add white chocolate and vanilla; stir 1 minute or until chocolate is melted and mixture is smooth. Stir in cherries and nuts.

Spread evenly in prepared pan. Score into 64 squares while fudge is still warm. Refrigerate until firm. Cut along score lines into squares.

Makes 64 candies

PEANUT BUTTER CHOCOLATE CHIPPERS

1 **cup creamy or chunky peanut butter**
1 **cup packed light brown sugar**
1 **large egg**
¾ **cup milk chocolate chips**
  Granulated sugar

1. Preheat oven to 350°F.

2. Combine peanut butter, brown sugar and egg in medium bowl; mix with mixing spoon until well blended. Add chips; mix well.

3. Roll heaping tablespoonfuls of dough into 1½-inch balls. Place balls 2 inches apart on ungreased cookie sheets.

4. Dip table fork into granulated sugar; press criss-cross fashion onto each ball, flattening to ½-inch thickness.

5. Bake 12 minutes or until set. Let cookies stand on cookie sheets 2 minutes. Remove cookies with spatula to wire racks; cool completely.   *Makes about 2 dozen cookies*

• •

Cook's Notes:
These simple-to-make cookies don't contain flour, resulting in a delicious, dense cookie.

• •

CHOCOLATE BUTTER CRUNCH

1 cup butter
1¼ cups sugar
¼ cup water
2 tablespoons light corn syrup
1 cup ground almonds, divided
½ teaspoon vanilla extract
¾ cup milk chocolate chips

Line 15½×10½×1-inch jelly-roll pan with foil, extending edges over sides of pan. Generously grease foil.

Melt butter in medium saucepan over medium heat. Add sugar, water and corn syrup. Bring to a boil, stirring constantly.

Attach candy thermometer to side of pan making sure bulb is submerged in sugar mixture but not touching bottom of pan. Cook until thermometer registers

290°F, stirring frequently. Stir in ⅔ cup almonds and vanilla. Pour into prepared pan. Spread mixture into corners with metal spatula. Let stand 1 minute. Sprinkle with chocolate chips. Let stand 2 to 3 minutes more until chocolate melts. Spread chocolate over candy. Sprinkle with remaining ⅓ cup almonds. Cool completely.

Lift candy out of pan using foil; remove foil. Break candy into pieces. Store in airtight container. *Makes about 1½ pounds*

QUICK CHOCOLATE SOFTIES

1 package (18.25 ounces) devil's food
  cake mix
⅓ cup water
¼ cup butter, softened
1 egg
1 cup white chocolate baking chips
½ cup coarsely chopped walnuts

1. Preheat oven to 350°F. Grease cookie
sheets.

2. Combine cake mix, water, butter and egg
in large bowl. Beat with
electric mixer at low speed
until moistened. Increase
speed to medium; beat 1
minute.

3. Stir in chips and nuts;
mix until well blended.

4. Drop dough by heaping
teaspoonfuls 2 inches
apart onto prepared
cookie sheets.

5. Bake 10 to 12 minutes or until set. Let
cookies stand on cookie sheets 1 minute.
Remove cookies to wire racks; cool
completely.   *Makes about 4 dozen cookies*

....

Cook's Notes:
For a more intense chocolate flavor,
substitute semisweet chocolate chips for the
white chocolate chips.

....

MINT TRUFFLES

1 **package (10 ounces) mint chocolate chips**
¹/₃ **cup whipping cream**
¹/₄ **cup butter**
1 **container (3½ ounces) chocolate sprinkles**

Line baking sheet with waxed paper; set aside. Melt chips with whipping cream and butter in medium saucepan over low heat, stirring occasionally. Pour into pie pan. Refrigerate until mixture is fudgy, but soft, about 2 hours.

Shape about 1 tablespoonful of mixture into 1¼-inch ball. To shape, roll mixture between palms. Repeat procedure with remaining mixture. Place balls on waxed paper.

Place sprinkles in shallow bowl; roll balls in sprinkles.

Place truffles in petit four or candy cups. (If sprinkles won't stick because truffle has set, roll truffle between palms until outside is soft.) Truffles may be refrigerated 2 to 3 days or frozen several weeks.

Makes about 24 truffles

Cook's Notes:

Truffles can be coated with unsweetened cocoa, powdered sugar, chopped nuts, sprinkles or cookie crumbs to add flavor and prevent the truffles from melting in your fingers.

ULTIMATE CHIPPERS

2½ **cups all-purpose flour**
1 **teaspoon baking soda**
½ **teaspoon salt**
1 **cup butter, softened**
1 **cup packed light brown sugar**
½ **cup granulated sugar**
2 **eggs**
1 **tablespoon vanilla**
1 **cup semisweet chocolate chips**
1 **cup milk chocolate chips**
1 **cup white chocolate baking chips**
½ **cup coarsely chopped pecans (optional)**

Preheat oven to 375°F. Combine flour, baking soda and salt in medium bowl. Set aside.

Beat butter and sugars in large bowl until light and fluffy. Beat in eggs and vanilla. Add flour mixture to butter mixture; beat until well blended. Stir in chips and pecans.

Drop by heaping teaspoonfuls 2 inches apart onto ungreased cookie sheets. Bake 10 to 12 minutes or until edges are golden brown. Let cookies stand on cookie sheets 2 minutes. Remove cookies to wire racks; cool completely. *Makes about 6 dozen cookies*

EASY EASEL RECIPES

DOUBLE-DECKER FUDGE

1 cup REESE'S® Peanut Butter Chips
1 cup HERSHEY'S Semi-Sweet Chocolate Chips or HERSHEY'S MINICHIPS™ Semi-Sweet Chocolate
2¼ cups sugar
1 jar (7 ounces) marshmallow creme
¾ cup evaporated milk
¼ cup (½ stick) butter or margarine
1 teaspoon vanilla extract

Line 8-inch square pan with foil, extending foil over edges of pan. In medium bowl, place peanut butter chips. In second medium bowl, place chocolate chips. In heavy 3-quart saucepan, combine sugar, marshmallow creme, evaporated milk and butter. Cook over medium heat, stirring constantly, until mixture comes to a boil; boil 5 minutes, stirring constantly. Remove from

heat; stir in vanilla. Immediately stir half of the hot mixture (1½ cups) into peanut butter chips until chips are completely melted; quickly spread into prepared pan. Stir remaining hot mixture into chocolate chips until chips are completely melted. Quickly spread over top of peanut butter layer. Cool to room temperature; refrigerate until firm. Use foil to lift fudge out of pan; peel off foil. Cut into 1-inch squares. Store in tightly covered container at room temperature.

Makes about 5 dozen pieces or about 2 pounds fudge

CHOCOLATE CRACKLETOPS

2 cups all-purpose flour
2 teaspoons baking powder
2 cups granulated sugar
½ cup (1 stick) butter or margarine
4 squares (1 ounce each) unsweetened baking chocolate, chopped
4 large eggs, lightly beaten
2 teaspoons vanilla extract
1¾ cups "M&M's"® Chocolate Mini Baking Bits
Additional granulated sugar

Combine flour and baking powder; set aside. In 2-quart saucepan over medium heat combine 2 cups sugar, butter and chocolate, stirring until butter and chocolate are melted; remove from heat. Gradually stir in eggs and vanilla. Stir in flour mixture until well blended. Chill mixture 1 hour. Stir in

"M&M's"® Chocolate Mini Baking Bits; chill mixture an additional 1 hour.

Preheat oven to 350°F. Line cookie sheets with foil. With sugar-dusted hands, roll dough into 1-inch balls; roll balls in additional granulated sugar. Place about 2 inches apart onto prepared cookie sheets. Bake 10 to 12 minutes. Do not overbake. Cool completely on wire racks. Store in tightly covered container.

Makes about 5 dozen cookies

EASY LUSCIOUS FUDGE

2 cups (12 ounces) semisweet chocolate chips

¾ cup milk chocolate chips

2 squares (1 ounce each) unsweetened chocolate, coarsely chopped

1 can (14 ounces) sweetened condensed milk

1 cup mini marshmallows

½ cup chopped walnuts (optional)

LINE 8-inch square pan with foil, extending 1 inch over ends of pan. Lightly grease foil.

MELT chocolates in medium saucepan over low heat, stirring constantly. Remove from heat. Stir in condensed milk; add marshmallows and walnuts, if desired, stirring until combined.

SPREAD chocolate mixture evenly in prepared pan. Score into 2-inch triangles by cutting halfway through fudge with sharp knife while fudge is still warm.

REFRIGERATE until firm. Remove from pan by lifting fudge and foil. Place on cutting board; cut along score lines into triangles. Remove foil. Store in airtight container in refrigerator.

Makes about 3 dozen pieces of fudge

Cook's Notes:

For Mint Fudge, substitute 1⅔ cups (10 ounces) mint chocolate chips for semisweet chips and ½ cup chopped party mints for walnuts.

BANANA CHOCOLATE CHIP SOFTIES

1¼ cups all-purpose flour
1 teaspoon baking powder
½ teaspoon salt
⅓ cup butter, softened
⅓ cup granulated sugar
⅓ cup packed light brown sugar
1 ripe, medium banana, mashed
1 large egg
1 teaspoon vanilla
1 cup milk chocolate chips
½ cup coarsely chopped walnuts (optional)

Preheat oven to 375°F. Lightly grease cookie sheets.

Place flour, baking powder and salt in small bowl; stir to combine.

Beat butter and sugars in large bowl with electric mixer at medium speed until light and fluffy. Beat in banana, egg and vanilla.

Add flour mixture. Beat at low speed until well blended. Stir in chips and walnuts. (Dough will be soft.)

Drop rounded teaspoonfuls of dough 2 inches apart onto prepared cookie sheets. Bake 9 to 11 minutes or until edges are golden brown. Let cookies stand on cookie sheets 2 minutes. Remove cookies to wire racks; cool completely.

Store tightly covered at room temperature. These cookies do not freeze well.

Makes about 3 dozen cookies

CHOCOLATE TORTONI

8 squares (1 ounce each) semi-sweet chocolate
⅔ cup KARO® Light or Dark Corn Syrup
2 cups heavy cream, divided
1½ cups broken chocolate wafer cookies
1 cup coarsely chopped walnuts
Chocolate, nuts and whipped cream (optional)

1. Line 12 (2½-inch) muffin pan cups with paper or foil liners.

2. In large heavy saucepan combine chocolate and corn syrup; stir over low heat just until chocolate melts. Remove from heat. Stir in ½ cup cream until blended.

3. Refrigerate 25 to 30 minutes or until cool. Stir in cookies and walnuts.

4. In small bowl with mixer at medium speed, beat remaining 1½ cups cream until soft peaks form; gently fold into chocolate mixture just until combined. Spoon into prepared muffin pan cups.

5. Freeze 4 hours or until firm. Let stand at room temperature several minutes before serving. If desired, garnish with chocolate, nuts or whipped cream. Store covered in freezer for up to 1 month.

Makes 12 servings

CHOCOLATE CHIP RUGALACH

1 cup (2 sticks) butter or margarine,
    slightly softened
2 cups all-purpose flour
1 cup vanilla ice cream, softened
½ cup strawberry jam
1 cup BAKER'S® Semi-Sweet Real
    Chocolate Chips
1 cup finely chopped nuts
    Powdered sugar

BEAT butter and flour. Beat in ice cream until well blended. Divide dough into 4 balls; wrap each in waxed paper. Refrigerate until firm, about 1 hour.

PREHEAT oven to 350°F. Roll dough, one ball at a time, on floured surface into 11×6-inch rectangle, about ⅛ inch thick. Spread with 2 tablespoons of the jam; sprinkle with ¼ cup of the chips and ¼ cup of the nuts. Roll up lengthwise as for jelly roll. Place on ungreased cookie sheet. Cut 12 diagonal slits in roll, being careful not to cut all the way through. Repeat with the remaining dough.

BAKE for 35 minutes or until golden brown. Cool 5 minutes on cookie sheet. Cut through each roll; separate pieces. Finish cooling on wire racks. Sprinkle with powdered sugar, if desired.   *Makes 4 dozen pieces*

Decadent Candies

Easy Turtle Fudge (page 121)

TINY MINI KISSES PEANUT BLOSSOMS

½ cup shortening
¾ cup REESE'S® Creamy Peanut Butter
⅓ cup granulated sugar
⅓ cup packed light brown sugar
1 egg
3 tablespoons milk
1 teaspoon vanilla extract
1½ cups all-purpose flour
½ teaspoon baking soda
½ teaspoon salt
Granulated sugar
HERSHEY'S MINI KISSES™ Chocolate

1. Heat oven to 350°F.

2. In large bowl, beat shortening and peanut butter with electric mixer until well mixed. Add ⅓ cup granulated sugar and brown sugar; beat well. Add egg, milk and vanilla; beat until fluffy. Stir together flour, baking soda and salt; gradually add to peanut butter mixture, beating until blended. Shape into ½-inch balls. Roll in granulated sugar; place on ungreased cookie sheet.

3. Bake 5 to 6 minutes or until set. Immediately press MINI KISS™ Chocolate into center of each cookie. Remove from cookie sheet to wire rack.

Makes about 14 dozen cookies

EASY EASEL RECIPES

CHOCOLATE RASPBERRY TRIFLE

CHOCOLATE CUSTARD

- 3 tablespoons cornstarch
- 1 tablespoon granulated sugar
- ⅛ teaspoon salt
- 2 cups milk
- 3 egg yolks
- 2 cups (11½-ounce package) NESTLÉ® TOLL HOUSE® Milk Chocolate Morsels, divided

TRIFLE

- 1 cup heavy whipping cream
- 1 tablespoon granulated sugar
- 1 (10¾ ounces) frozen pound cake, thawed
- 2 tablespoons crème de cacao, divided
- ¼ cup seedless raspberry jam
  Raspberries and NESTLÉ® Cocoa (optional)

FOR CHOCOLATE CUSTARD:

COMBINE cornstarch, sugar and salt in medium, heavy saucepan. Gradually add milk. Whisk in egg yolks until smooth. Cook over medium heat, stirring constantly, until mixture comes to a boil; boil for 1 minute. Remove from heat. Add *1½ cups* morsels; stir until melted and smooth. Press plastic wrap on surface; chill.

FOR TRIFLE:

BEAT cream and sugar until stiff peaks form. Cut cake into ½-inch-thick slices. Cut one slice into thin strips; reserve for top. In 2-quart straight sided bowl, layer ½ cake slices, ½ crème de cacao, ½ jam, ½ chocolate custard and ½ whipping cream. Repeat cake, créme de cacao, jam and chocolate custard layers. Top with reserved cake strips, *¼ cup* morsels, remaining whipped cream and *remaining* morsels. Chill. Garnish with raspberries and sprinkle with cocoa.

Cookie Jar Favorites

Chocolate-Dipped Orange Logs (page 23)

CHOCOLATE DESSERT TIMBALES

1 envelope unflavored gelatin
½ cup cold water
⅓ cup sugar
3 tablespoons HERSHEY'S Cocoa
1½ cups lowfat milk, 1% milkfat
2 egg yolks, slightly beaten
2 teaspoons vanilla extract
1 cup frozen light non-dairy whipped topping, thawed
Whipped topping
Fresh raspberries or canned fruit slices, drained

In small bowl, sprinkle gelatin over cold water; let stand several minutes to soften. In medium saucepan, stir together sugar and cocoa; gradually stir in milk. Stir in egg yolks. Cook over medium heat, stirring constantly, until mixture just begins to boil; remove from heat. Stir in reserved gelatin mixture and vanilla; stir until gelatin is completely dissolved.

Transfer to medium bowl; refrigerate, stirring occasionally, until mixture begins to set. Carefully fold 1 cup whipped topping into chocolate mixture, blending until smooth. Pour into 6 small serving dishes or custard cups; refrigerate until set. Garnish with whipped topping and fruit.

Makes 6 servings

TOFFEE CHUNK BROWNIE COOKIES

1 cup butter
4 ounces unsweetened chocolate,
   coarsely chopped
1½ cups sugar
2 eggs
1 tablespoon vanilla
3 cups all-purpose flour
⅛ teaspoon salt
1½ cups coarsely chopped chocolate-
   covered toffee bars

PREHEAT oven to 350°F. Melt butter and chocolate in large saucepan over low heat, stirring until smooth. Remove from heat; cool slightly.

STIR sugar into chocolate mixture until smooth. Stir in eggs until well blended. Stir in vanilla until smooth.

Stir in flour and salt just until mixed. Fold in toffee.

DROP heaping tablespoonfuls of dough 1½ inches apart onto ungreased cookie sheets.

BAKE 12 minutes or until just set. Let cookies stand on cookie sheets 5 minutes; transfer to wire racks to cool completely. Store in airtight container.

Makes 36 cookies

CHOCOLATE–RUM PARFAITS

6 to 6½ ounces Mexican chocolate,
    coarsely chopped*
1½ cups heavy or whipping cream, divided
3 tablespoons golden rum (optional)
¾ teaspoon vanilla extract
    Additional whipped cream, for garnish
    Sliced almonds, for garnish
    Cookies (optional)

*Or, substitute 6 ounces semi-sweet chocolate,
coarsely chopped, 1 tablespoon ground
cinnamon and ¼ teaspoon almond extract for
Mexican chocolate.*

Combine chocolate and 3 tablespoons cream in top of double boiler. Heat over simmering water until smooth, stirring occasionally. Gradually stir in rum, if desired; remove top pan from heat. Let stand at room temperature 15 minutes to cool slightly.

Combine remaining cream and vanilla in chilled small bowl. Beat with electric mixer at low speed, then gradually increase speed until stiff but not dry peaks form.

Gently fold whipped cream into cooled chocolate mixture until uniform in color. Spoon mousse into 4 individual dessert dishes. Refrigerate 2 to 3 hours until firm. Garnish with additional whipped cream and sliced almonds. Serve with cookies, if desired.   *Makes 4 servings*

CHOCOLATE–DIPPED ORANGE LOGS

3¼ cups all-purpose flour
⅓ teaspoon salt
1 cup butter, softened
1 cup sugar
2 eggs
1½ teaspoons grated orange peel
1 teaspoon vanilla
1 package (12 ounces) semisweet
   chocolate chips
1½ cups pecan pieces, finely chopped

COMBINE flour and salt in medium bowl. Beat butter in large bowl with electric mixer at medium speed until smooth. Gradually beat in sugar; increase speed to high and beat until light and fluffy. Beat in eggs, 1 at a time, blending well after each addition. Beat in orange peel and vanilla until blended. Gradually stir in flour mixture until blended. (Dough will be crumbly.)

GATHER dough together and press gently to form a ball. Flatten into disk; wrap in plastic wrap and refrigerate 2 hours or until firm.

PREHEAT oven to 350°F. Shape dough into 1-inch balls. Roll balls on flat surface with fingertips to form 3-inch logs about ½ inch thick. Place logs 1 inch apart on ungreased cookie sheets.

BAKE 17 minutes or until bottoms of cookies are golden brown. (Cookies will feel soft and look white on top; they will become crisp when cool.) Transfer to wire racks to cool completely.

MELT chocolate chips in medium saucepan over low heat. Place chopped pecans on sheet of waxed paper. Dip one end of each cookie in chocolate, shaking off excess. Roll chocolate-covered ends in pecans. Place on waxed paper-lined cookie sheets and let stand until chocolate is set, or refrigerate about 5 minutes to set chocolate.

Makes about 36 cookies

CHOCOLATE MOUSSE ESPRESSO

- **2 envelopes KNOX® Unflavored Gelatine**
- **¾ cup sugar, divided**
- **4 teaspoons instant espresso coffee powder**
- **2¾ cups milk**
- **12 squares (1 ounce each) semisweet chocolate**
- **1½ cups heavy cream**
- **45 NABISCO ® FAMOUS Chocolate Wafers**
- **⅔ cup hazelnuts, toasted**

Combine gelatine with ½ cup sugar and coffee powder in medium saucepan. Stir in milk. Let stand without stirring 3 minutes for gelatine to soften. Heat over low heat, stirring constantly, until gelatine is completely dissolved, about 5 minutes.

Add chocolate and continue heating over low heat, stirring constantly, until chocolate is melted. Using wire whisk, beat until chocolate is thoroughly blended. Pour into large bowl and refrigerate, stirring occasionally. Chill until mixture mounds slightly when dropped from spoon. Remove from refrigerator.

Pour chilled whipping cream and remaining ¼ cup sugar into chilled bowl and beat with electric mixer at high speed until soft peaks form. Reserve ½ cup for garnish. Gently fold remaining whipped cream into gelatine mixture.

Place cookies and hazelnuts in food processor or blender container; process with on/off pulses until finely crushed.

Alternately layer gelatine mixture with cookie crumb mixture in dessert dishes. Refrigerate at least 30 minutes. Garnish, if desired.   *Makes about 10 servings*

COCOA PECAN CRESCENTS

1 cup (2 sticks) butter or margarine, softened
⅔ cup granulated sugar
1½ teaspoons vanilla extract
1¾ cups all-purpose flour
⅓ cup HERSHEY'S Cocoa
⅛ teaspoon salt
1½ cups ground pecans
Powdered sugar

In large mixer bowl, beat butter, granulated sugar and vanilla until light and fluffy. Stir together flour, cocoa and salt. Add to butter mixture; blend well. Stir in pecans.

Refrigerate dough 1 hour or until firm enough to handle. Heat oven to 375°F. Shape scant 1 tablespoon dough into log about 2½ inches long; place on ungreased cookie sheet. Shape each log into crescent, tapering ends.

Bake 13 to 15 minutes or until set. Cool slightly; remove from cookie sheet to wire rack. Cool completely. Roll in powdered sugar. *Makes about 3½ dozen cookies*

CHOCOLATE FONDUE

⅔ **cup KARO® Light or Dark Corn Syrup**
½ **cup heavy cream**
 8 **squares (1 ounce each) semisweet**
    chocolate
 Assorted fresh fruit

1. In medium saucepan combine corn syrup and cream. Bring to boil over medium heat.

2. Remove from heat. Add chocolate; stir until completely melted.

3. Serve warm as a dip for fruit.
Makes 1½ cups fondue

Microwave Directions: In medium microwavable bowl combine corn syrup and cream. Microwave on HIGH (100%), 1½ minutes or until boiling. Add chocolate; stir until completely melted. Serve as directed.

Cook's Notes:
Chocolate Fondue can be made a day ahead. Store covered in refrigerator. Reheat before serving.

Serve it with Style:
Try some of these dippers: candied pineapple, dried apricots, waffle squares, ladyfingers, macaroons, pretzels, croissants, mint cookies or peanut butter cookies.

CHOCOLATE PECAN TASSIES

CRUST
- ½ cup (1 stick) margarine or butter
- 1 package (3 ounces) PHILADELPHIA BRAND® Cream Cheese, softened
- 1 cup all-purpose flour

FILLING
- 1 square BAKER'S® Unsweetened Chocolate
- 1 tablespoon margarine or butter
- ¾ cup packed brown sugar
- 1 egg
- 1 teaspoon vanilla extract
- 1 cup chopped pecans
  Powdered sugar (optional)

• **BEAT** ½ cup margarine and cream cheese until well blended. Beat in flour until just blended. Wrap dough in plastic wrap; refrigerate 1 hour.

• **HEAT** oven to 350°F. Microwave chocolate and 1 tablespoon margarine in large microwavable bowl on HIGH 1 minute or until margarine is melted. Stir until chocolate is completely melted.

• **BEAT** in brown sugar, egg and vanilla until thickened. Stir in pecans.

• **SHAPE** chilled dough into 36 (1-inch) balls. Flatten each ball and press onto bottoms and up sides of ungreased miniature muffin cups. Spoon about 1 teaspoon filling into each cup.

• **BAKE** 20 minutes. Cool in pans on wire racks 15 minutes. Remove from pans. Sprinkle with powdered sugar.

Makes 36 tassies

EASY EASEL RECIPES

TWO GREAT TASTES PUDDING PARFAITS

1 **package (4¾ ounces) vanilla pudding and pie filling**
3½ **cups milk**
1 **cup REESE'S® Peanut Butter Chips**
1 **cup HERSHEY'S® Semi-Sweet Chocolate Chips**
   Whipped topping (optional)

In large, heavy saucepan combine pudding mix and 3½ cups milk (rather than amount listed in package directions). Cook over medium heat, stirring constantly, until mixture comes to full boil. Remove from heat; divide hot mixture between 2 heat-proof medium bowls. Immediately stir peanut butter chips into mixture in one bowl and chocolate chips into mixture in second bowl. Stir both mixtures until melted and smooth. Cool slightly, stirring occasionally. Alternately spoon peanut butter and chocolate mixtures into parfait glasses, champagne glasses or dessert dishes. Place plastic wrap directly onto surface of each dessert; refrigerate several hours or overnight. Top with whipped topping and garnish as desired.

Makes 4 to 6 servings

NUTTY CLUSTERS

2 squares (1 ounce each) unsweetened
   chocolate
½ cup butter, softened
1 cup sugar
1 egg
⅓ cup buttermilk
1 teaspoon vanilla
1¾ cups all-purpose flour
½ teaspoon baking soda
1 cup mixed salted nuts, coarsely
   chopped
Easy Chocolate Icing (recipe follows)

Preheat oven to 400°F. Line cookie sheets
with parchment paper or leave ungreased.

Melt chocolate in top of double boiler over
hot, not boiling, water. Remove from heat;
cool. Beat butter and sugar in large bowl
until smooth. Beat in egg, melted chocolate,
buttermilk and vanilla until light. Stir in
flour and baking soda just until blended. Stir
in nuts. Drop dough by teaspoonfuls 2 inches
apart onto cookie sheets.

Bake 8 to 10 minutes or until almost no
imprint remains when touched. Immediately
remove cookies from cookie sheets to wire
racks. While cookies bake, prepare Easy
Chocolate Icing. Frost cookies while still
warm.   *Makes about 4 dozen cookies*

Easy Chocolate Icing

2 squares (1 ounce each) unsweetened
   chocolate
2 tablespoons butter
2 cups powdered sugar
2 to 3 tablespoons water

Melt chocolate and butter in small saucepan
over low heat, stirring until completely
melted. Add powdered sugar and water; mix
until smooth.

STRIPED DELIGHT

1 cup flour
1 cup finely chopped pecans
¼ cup sugar (optional)
½ cup (1 stick) butter or margarine, melted
1 package (8 ounces) PHILADELPHIA BRAND® Cream Cheese, softened
¼ cup sugar
2 tablespoons milk
1 tub (8 ounces) COOL WHIP® Whipped Topping, thawed
3½ cups cold milk
2 packages (4-serving size) JELL-O® Chocolate Flavor Instant Pudding & Pie Filling

HEAT oven to 350°F.

MIX flour, pecans and ¼ cup sugar in 13×9-inch baking pan. Stir in butter until flour is moistened.

Press firmly onto bottom of pan. Bake 20 minutes or until lightly browned. Cool.

BEAT cream cheese, ¼ cup sugar and 2 tablespoons milk in large bowl with wire whisk until smooth. Gently stir in ½ of the whipped topping. Spread onto cooled crust.

POUR 3½ cups milk into large bowl. Add pudding mixes. Beat with wire whisk 1 to 2 minutes or until well blended. Pour over cream cheese layer.

REFRIGERATE 4 hours or until set. Just before serving, spread remaining whipped topping over pudding. Garnish as desired.

Makes 15 servings

RASPBERRY-FILLED CHOCOLATE RAVIOLI

2 squares (1 ounce each) bittersweet or
    semisweet chocolate
1 cup butter, softened
½ cup sugar
1 egg
1 teaspoon vanilla
½ teaspoon chocolate extract
¼ teaspoon baking soda
    Dash salt
2½ cups all-purpose flour
1 to 1¼ cups seedless raspberry jam
    Powdered sugar

Melt chocolate in top of double boiler over hot, not boiling, water. Remove from heat; cool. Mix butter and sugar in large bowl until blended. Add melted chocolate, egg, vanilla, chocolate extract, baking soda and salt; beat until light. Blend in flour. Divide dough in half. Cover; refrigerate until firm.

Preheat oven to 350°F. Lightly grease cookie sheets. Roll out dough, half at a time, ⅛-inch thick between two sheets of plastic wrap. Remove top sheet of plastic. Cut dough into 1½-inch squares. Place half of the squares, 2 inches apart, on prepared cookie sheets. Place about ½ teaspoon jam on center of each square; top with another square. Using fork, press edges of squares together to seal, then pierce center of each square. Bake 10 minutes or just until edges are browned. Remove to wire racks to cool. Dust lightly with powdered sugar.

Makes about 6 dozen ravioli

COCOA CAPPUCCINO MOUSSE

1 can (14 ounces) sweetened condensed
  milk (not evaporated milk)
⅓ cup HERSHEY'S Cocoa
3 tablespoons butter or margarine
2 teaspoons powdered instant coffee or
  espresso, dissolved in 2 teaspoons
  hot water
2 cups (1 pint) cold whipping cream

1. Combine sweetened condensed milk,
cocoa, butter and coffee in medium
saucepan. Cook over low heat, stirring
constantly, until butter
melts and mixture is
smooth. Remove from
heat; cool.

2. Beat whipping cream
in large bowl until stiff.
Gradually fold chocolate
mixture into whipped
cream. Spoon into dessert

dishes. Refrigerate until set, about 2 hours.
Garnish as desired.   *Makes 8 servings*

. . . .

Cook's Notes:
*For best results when beating whipping cream,
chill the cream, bowl and beaters first—the cold
keeps the fat in the cream solid, thus increasing the
volume. For optimum volume, beat the cream in a
deep narrow bowl.*

. . . .

HOLIDAY CHOCOLATE SHORTBREAD COOKIES

1 cup (2 sticks) butter, softened
1¼ cups powdered sugar
1 teaspoon vanilla extract
½ cup HERSHEY'S Dutch Processed Cocoa or HERSHEY'S Cocoa
1¾ cups all-purpose flour
1⅔ cups (10-ounce package) HERSHEY'S Premier White Chips

1. Heat oven to 300°F. Beat butter, powdered sugar and vanilla in large bowl until creamy. Add cocoa; beat until well blended. Gradually add flour, stirring until smooth.

2. Roll or pat dough to ¼-inch thickness on lightly floured surface or between 2 pieces of wax paper. Cut into holiday shapes using star, tree, wreath or other cookie cutters. Reroll dough scraps, cutting cookies until dough is used. Place on ungreased cookie sheet.

3. Bake 15 to 20 minutes or just until firm. Immediately place white chips, flat side down, in decorative design on warm cookies. Cool slightly; remove from cookie sheet to wire rack. Cool completely.
Makes about 4½ dozen (2-inch diameter) cookies

Cook's Notes:
For more even baking, place similar shapes and sizes of cookies on same cookie sheet.

Creamy Creations

Two Great Tastes Pudding Parfaits (page 104)

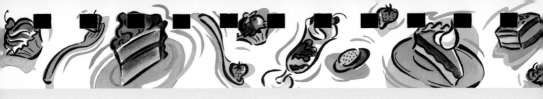

COCOA CRINKLE SANDWICHES

1¾ **cups all-purpose flour**
 ½ **cup unsweetened cocoa powder**
 1 **teaspoon baking soda**
 ¼ **teaspoon salt**
 ½ **cup butter**
1¾ **cups sugar, divided**
 2 **eggs**
 2 **teaspoons vanilla**
 1 **can (16 ounces) chocolate frosting**
 ½ **cup crushed candy canes* (optional)**

*To crush candy canes, place candy in sealed heavy-duty plastic food storage bag. Crush into small pieces with a heavy object such as a meat mallet or rolling pin.

COMBINE flour, cocoa, baking soda and salt in medium bowl.

MELT butter in large saucepan over medium heat; cool slightly. Add 1¼ cups sugar; whisk until smooth. Whisk in eggs, 1 at a time, until blended. Stir in vanilla until smooth. Stir in flour mixture just until combined.

Wrap dough in plastic wrap; refrigerate 2 hours.

PREHEAT oven to 350°F. Grease cookie sheets. Shape dough into 1-inch balls. Place remaining ½ cup sugar in shallow bowl; roll balls in sugar. Place 1½ inches apart on cookie sheets.

BAKE 12 minutes or until cookies feel set to the touch. Let cookies stand on cookie sheets 5 minutes; transfer to wire racks to cool completely.

STIR frosting until soft and smooth. Place crushed candy canes on piece of waxed paper. Spread about 2 teaspoons frosting over flat side of one cookie. Place second cookie, flat side down, over frosting, pressing down to allow frosting to squeeze out slightly between cookies. Press exposed frosting into crushed candy canes. Repeat with remaining cookies. *Makes about 20 sandwich cookies*

CHOCOLATE DELIGHT

½ **cup granulated sugar**
2 **tablespoons cornstarch**
3 **egg yolks**
1 **cup milk**
3 **bars (6 ounces) NESTLÉ® Unsweetened Baking Chocolate, broken up**
3 **tablespoons almond-flavored liqueur**
48 **(two 3-ounce packages) ladyfingers**
1½ **cups heavy or whipping cream**
1 **cup powdered sugar**
   Sweetened whipped cream (optional)
   Chocolate curls (optional)

COMBINE sugar and cornstarch in 2-quart saucepan. Whisk in egg yolks and milk. Cook over medium-low heat, stirring constantly with wire whisk, until mixture boils; boil for 1 minute, whisking constantly. Add

baking bars; whisk until mixture is smooth. Whisk in liqueur. Press plastic wrap directly on surface of chocolate mixture. Cool to room temperature.

LINE side of 9-inch springform pan with ladyfingers, cut sides in. Arrange half of remaining ladyfingers on bottom of pan.

BEAT cream and powdered sugar in small mixer bowl until stiff peaks form. Stir chocolate mixture until smooth; fold in whipped cream. Spoon half of chocolate mixture into pan. Layer with remaining ladyfingers and chocolate mixture. Cover; chill for 4 hours or overnight. Remove rim; garnish with whipped cream and chocolate curls.

Makes 10 to 12 servings

EASY EASEL RECIPES

CHOCOLATE-DIPPED CINNAMON THINS

1¼ **cups all-purpose flour**
1½ **teaspoons ground cinnamon**
¼ **teaspoon salt**
1 **cup butter, softened**
1 **cup powdered sugar**
1 **large egg**
1 **teaspoon vanilla**
4 **ounces broken bittersweet chocolate, chopped**

1. Place flour, cinnamon and salt in small bowl; stir to combine.

2. Beat butter in large bowl with electric mixer at medium speed until light and fluffy. Add sugar; beat well. Add egg and vanilla; beat well. Gradually add flour mixture; beat at low speed.

3. Place dough on sheet of waxed paper. Using waxed paper to hold dough, roll it back and forth to form a log about 12 inches long and 2½ inches wide.

4. Wrap log in plastic wrap. Refrigerate at least 2 hours or until firm.

5. Preheat oven to 350°F. Cut dough into ¼-inch-thick slices. Place 2 inches apart on ungreased cookie sheets.

6. Bake 10 minutes or until set. Let cookies stand on cookie sheets 2 minutes. Remove to wire racks; cool completely.

7. Melt chocolate in small saucepan over low heat, stirring constantly.

8. Dip each cookie into chocolate, coating 1 inch up sides. Let excess chocolate drip back into saucepan.

9. Transfer to wire racks or waxed paper; let stand at cool room temperature about 40 minutes until chocolate is set.

Makes about 2 dozen cookies

DOUBLE LAYER CHOCOLATE PIE

4 ounces PHILADELPHIA BRAND®
  Cream Cheese, softened
1 tablespoon milk or half-and-half
1 tablespoon sugar
1 tub (8 ounces) COOL WHIP® Whipped
  Topping, thawed
1 prepared chocolate flavor crumb crust
  (6 ounces)
2 cups cold milk or half-and-half
2 packages (4-serving size) JELL-O®
  Chocolate Flavor Instant Pudding &
  Pie Filling

Beat with wire whisk until well mixed.
(Mixture will be thick.) Immediately stir in
remaining whipped topping. Spread over
cream cheese layer.

REFRIGERATE 4 hours or until set.
Garnish as desired.   *Makes 8 servings*

....

Cook's Notes:
*To soften cream cheese quickly, microwave on high
for 15 to 20 seconds.*

....

MIX cream cheese, 1
tablespoon milk and sugar
in large bowl with wire
whisk until smooth.
Gently stir in 1½ cups of
the whipped topping.
Spread onto bottom of
crust.

POUR 2 cups milk into
bowl. Add pudding mixes.

CHOCOLATE SUGAR SPRITZ

**2 squares (1 ounce each) unsweetened
    chocolate, coarsely chopped**
2¼ cups all-purpose flour
¼ teaspoon salt
1 cup butter, softened
¾ cup granulated sugar
1 large egg
1 teaspoon almond extract
½ cup powdered sugar
1 teaspoon ground cinnamon

1. Preheat oven to 400°F. Melt chocolate in
small saucepan over low
heat, stirring constantly;
set aside.

2. Combine flour and salt
in small bowl; set aside.

3. Beat butter and
granulated sugar in large
bowl with electric mixer
at medium speed until
light and fluffy. Beat in

egg and almond extract. Beat in chocolate.
Gradually stir in flour mixture with mixing
spoon. (Dough will be stiff.)

4. Fit cookie press with desired plate. Fill
press with dough; press dough 1 inch apart
onto ungreased cookie sheets. Bake 7
minutes or until just set.

5. Combine powdered sugar and cinnamon
in small bowl. Transfer to fine-mesh strainer
and sprinkle over hot cookies while they are
still on cookie sheets.
Remove cookies to wire
racks; cool completely.
Makes 4 to 5 dozen cookies

FUDGY BITTERSWEET BROWNIE PIE

12 ounces bittersweet chocolate candy bar, broken into pieces
½ cup butter
2 large eggs
½ cup sugar
1 cup all-purpose flour
½ teaspoon salt
Vanilla ice cream
Prepared hot fudge sauce
Red and white candy sprinkles for garnish

1. Preheat oven to 350°F. Grease 10-inch tart pan with removable bottom or 9-inch square baking pan; set aside. Melt chocolate and butter in small saucepan over low heat, stirring constantly; set aside.

2. Beat eggs in medium bowl with electric mixer at medium speed 30 seconds. Gradually beat in sugar; beat 1 minute. Beat in chocolate mixture. Beat in flour and salt at low speed until just combined. Spread batter evenly in prepared baking pan. Bake 25 minutes or until center is just set. Remove pan to wire rack; cool completely.

3. To serve, cut brownies into 12 wedges, or 12 squares if using square pan. Top each piece with a scoop of vanilla ice cream. Place fudge sauce in small microwavable bowl. Microwave at HIGH until hot, stirring once. Spoon over ice cream; top with candy sprinkles, if desired. *Makes 16 brownies*

ALMOND CRESCENTS

1 cup butter, softened
⅓ cup sugar
1¾ cups all-purpose flour
¼ cup cornstarch
1 teaspoon vanilla extract
1½ cups ground almonds
　Chocolate Glaze (recipe follows)

Preheat oven to 325°F.

Beat butter and granulated sugar in large bowl until creamy. Mix in flour, cornstarch and vanilla. Stir in almonds.

Shape tablespoonfuls of dough into crescents. Place 2 inches apart on ungreased cookie sheets.

Bake 22 to 25 minutes or until light brown. Cool 1 minute. Remove to wire racks; cool completely. Drizzle with Chocolate Glaze. Allow chocolate to set, then store in airtight container.

Makes about 3 dozen cookies

Chocolate Glaze: Place ½ cup semisweet chocolate chips and 1 tablespoon butter or margarine in small resealable plastic bag. Place bag in bowl of hot water for 2 to 3 minutes or until chocolate is softened. Dry with paper towel. Knead until chocolate mixture is smooth. Cut off very tiny corner of bag. Drizzle chocolate mixture over cookies.

HERSHEY'S COCOA CREAM PIE

1¼ cups sugar
½ cup HERSHEY'S Cocoa
⅓ cup cornstarch
¼ teaspoon salt
3 cups milk
3 tablespoons butter or margarine
1½ teaspoons vanilla extract
1 baked 9-inch pie crust or graham cracker crumb crust, cooled

In medium saucepan, stir together sugar, cocoa, cornstarch and salt. Gradually add milk, stirring until smooth. Cook over medium heat, stirring constantly, until mixture comes to a boil. Boil 1 minute. Remove from heat; stir in butter and vanilla.

Pour into prepared crust. Press plastic wrap directly onto surface. Cool to room temperature. Refrigerate 6 to 8 hours. Garnish as desired. Cover; refrigerate leftover pie. *Makes 6 to 8 servings*

Cook's Notes:

Cornstarch is a smooth powder made from corn. It is most often used as a thickening agent, but is also used in combination with flour in some cookie and cake recipes to create a more delicate texture.

CHOCOLATE MACAROONS

1 can (8 ounces) almond paste
2 large egg whites
½ cup powdered sugar
12 ounces semisweet chocolate chips, melted
2 tablespoons all-purpose flour
Powdered sugar (optional)

Preheat oven to 300°F. Line cookie sheets with parchment paper; set aside.

Beat almond paste, egg whites and sugar in large bowl with electric mixer at medium speed for 1 minute. Beat in chocolate until well combined. Beat in flour at low speed.

Spoon dough into pastry tube fitted with rosette tip. Pipe 1½-inch spirals 1 inch apart onto prepared cookie sheets. Pipe all cookies at once; dough will get stiff upon standing.

Bake 20 minutes or until set. Carefully remove parchment paper to countertop; cool completely.

Peel cookies off parchment paper. Sprinkle powdered sugar over cookies, if desired.

Makes about 3 dozen cookies

JUBILEE PIE

3 eggs
1 cup milk
½ cup **KARO® Light or Dark Corn Syrup**
½ cup baking mix
2 tablespoons sugar
2 cups (12 ounces) semi-sweet chocolate chips, melted
1 can (21 ounces) cherry pie filling
¼ teaspoon almond extract
1 cup heavy or whipping cream, whipped

1. Preheat oven to 350°F. Spray 9-inch pie plate with Mazola No Stick® cooking spray.

2. In blender or food processor blend first 6 ingredients 1 minute. Pour into pie plate; let stand 5 minutes.

3. Bake 35 to 40 minutes or until filling is puffed and set. Cool on wire rack; center will fall, forming a "well."

4. Combine cherry pie filling and almond extract; spoon into "well" in pie. Top with whipped cream. *Makes 8 servings*

EASY EASEL RECIPES

PECAN MINI KISS CUPS

½ cup (1 stick) butter or margarine, softened
1 package (3 ounces) cream cheese, softened
1 cup all-purpose flour
1 egg
⅔ cup packed light brown sugar
1 tablespoon butter, melted
1 teaspoon vanilla extract
   Dash salt
72 HERSHEY'S MINI KISSES™ Chocolate, divided
½ to ¾ cup coarsely chopped pecans

1. Beat ½ cup softened butter and cream cheese in medium bowl until blended. Add flour; beat well. Cover; refrigerate about 1 hour or until firm enough to handle.

2. Heat oven to 325°F. Stir together egg, brown sugar, 1 tablespoon melted butter, vanilla and salt in small bowl until well blended.

3. Shape chilled dough into 24 balls (1 inch each). Place balls in ungreased small muffin cups (1¾ inches in diameter). Press onto bottom and up side of cups. Place 2 MINI KISSES™ in each cup. Spoon about 1 teaspoon pecans over chocolate. Fill each cup with egg mixture.

4. Bake 25 minutes or until filling is set. Lightly press 1 MINI KISS™ into center of each cookie. Cool in pan on wire rack.
Makes 24 cups

CHOCOLATE RASPBERRY TART

1 package (4-serving size) JELL-O® Pudding and Pie Filling, Vanilla Flavor

1¾ cups half and half or milk Chocolate Crumb Crust (recipe follows), baked in 9-inch tart pan and cooled

1 pint raspberries

2 squares BAKER'S® Semi-Sweet Chocolate, melted

Microwave pie filling mix and half and half in large microwavable bowl on HIGH 3 minutes; stir well. Microwave 3 minutes longer; stir again. Microwave 1 minute or until mixture comes to a boil. Cover surface with plastic wrap. Refrigerate at least 4 hours.

Spoon filling into Chocolate Crumb Crust just before serving. Arrange raspberries on top of filling. Drizzle with melted chocolate.

Makes 8 to 10 servings

Saucepan Preparation: Combine pie filling mix and half and half in 2-quart saucepan. Cook over medium heat until mixture comes to a full boil, stirring constantly. Continue as directed.

Chocolate Crumb Crust

3 squares BAKER'S® Semi-Sweet Chocolate

3 tablespoons margarine or butter

1 cup graham cracker crumbs

Heat oven to 375°F.

Microwave chocolate and margarine in microwavable bowl on HIGH 2 minutes or until margarine is melted. Stir until chocolate is completely melted.

Stir in crumbs. Press mixture onto bottom and up sides of 9-inch tart pan or pie plate. Freeze 10 minutes. Bake for 8 minutes. Cool on wire rack.

Makes one 9-inch crust

Killer Brownies

Minted Chocolate Chip Brownies (page 43)

MINI CHOCOLATE PIES

1 package (4-serving size) chocolate
   cook & serve pudding and pie filling
   mix*
1 cup HERSHEY'S MINICHIPS™
   Semi-Sweet Chocolate
1 package (4 ounces) single serve
   graham cracker crusts (6 crusts)
   Whipped topping
   Additional MINICHIPS™ Semi-Sweet
   Chocolate

*Do not use instant pudding mix.

1. Prepare pudding and
pie filling mix as directed
on package; remove from
heat. Immediately add 1
cup small chocolate chips;
stir until melted. Cool 5
minutes, stirring
occasionally.

2. Pour filling into crusts;
press plastic wrap directly

onto surface. Refrigerate several hours or
until firm. Garnish with whipped topping
and small chocolate chips.

Makes 6 servings

Cook's Notes:
*Bloom, the gray-white film that sometimes
appears on chocolate and chocolate chips, occurs
when chocolate is exposed to varying temperatures
or has been stored in damp conditions. Bloom does
not affect the taste or quality of the chocolate.*

EASY EASEL RECIPES

ONE BOWL® BROWNIES

4 squares BAKER'S® Unsweetened Chocolate
¾ cup (1½ sticks) margarine or butter
2 cups sugar
3 eggs
1 teaspoon vanilla
1 cup flour
1 cup chopped nuts (optional)

HEAT oven to 350°F (325°F for glass baking dish). Line 13×9-inch baking pan with foil extending over edges to form handles. Grease foil.

MICROWAVE chocolate and margarine in large microwavable bowl on HIGH 2 minutes or until margarine is melted. Stir until chocolate is completely melted.

STIR sugar into chocolate until well blended. Mix in

eggs and vanilla. Stir in flour and nuts until well blended. Spread in prepared pan.

BAKE 30 to 35 minutes or until toothpick inserted into center comes out with fudgy crumbs. Do not overbake. Cool in pan. Lift out of pan onto cutting board. Cut into squares. *Makes 24 fudgy brownies*

Top of Stove Preparation: Melt chocolate and margarine in heavy 3-quart saucepan on very low heat, stirring constantly. Remove from heat. Continue as directed.

GERMAN SWEET CHOCOLATE PIE

1 package (4 ounces) BAKER'S®
   GERMAN'S Sweet Chocolate
⅓ cup milk, divided
4 ounces PHILADELPHIA BRAND®
   Cream Cheese, cubed, softened
2 tablespoons sugar
1 tub (8 ounces) COOL WHIP® Whipped
   Topping, thawed
1 prepared graham cracker crumb crust
   (6 ounces)
   Additional COOL WHIP® Whipped
   Topping, thawed
   Shaved chocolate

MICROWAVE chocolate
and 2 tablespoons milk in
large microwavable bowl
on HIGH 1½ to 2 minutes
or until chocolate is almost
melted, stirring halfway
through heating time. Stir
until chocolate is
completely melted.

BEAT cream cheese, sugar and remaining
milk into chocolate with wire whisk until
well blended. Refrigerate about 10 minutes
to cool. Gently stir in 1 tub whipped topping
until smooth. Spoon into crust.

FREEZE 4 hours or until firm. Let stand at
room temperature 15 minutes before serving
or until pie can be cut easily. Garnish with
additional whipped topping and shaved
chocolate.   *Makes 8 servings*

IRISH BROWNIES

4 squares (1 ounce each) semisweet chocolate, coarsely chopped
½ cup plus 2 tablespoons butter, divided
½ cup sugar
2 eggs
¼ cup plus 2 tablespoons Irish cream liqueur, divided
1 cup all-purpose flour
½ teaspoon baking powder
¼ teaspoon salt
2 ounces cream cheese, softened
1½ cups powdered sugar

Preheat oven to 350°F. Grease 8-inch square baking pan.

Melt chocolate and ½ cup butter in medium saucepan over low heat, stirring constantly. Remove from heat. Stir in sugar. Beat in eggs, 1 at a time, with wire whisk. Whisk in ¼ cup Irish cream. Combine flour, baking powder and salt in small bowl; stir into chocolate mixture until just blended. Spread batter evenly in prepared pan. Bake 22 to 25 minutes or until center is set. Remove pan to wire rack; cool completely.

Meanwhile, beat cream cheese and remaining 2 tablespoons butter in small bowl with electric mixer at medium speed until smooth. Beat in remaining 2 tablespoons Irish cream. Gradually beat in powdered sugar until smooth.

Spread frosting over cooled brownies. Chill at least 1 hour or until frosting is set. Cut into 2-inch squares.
Makes about 16 brownies

PEANUT–BUTTER–BANANA BROWNIE PIZZA

1 package (21½ ounces) brownie mix
1 package (8 ounces) PHILADELPHIA BRAND® Cream Cheese, softened
¼ cup sugar
¼ cup creamy peanut butter
3 large bananas, peeled, sliced
¼ cup coarsely chopped peanuts
2 squares BAKER'S® Semi-Sweet Chocolate
2 teaspoons butter or margarine

PREPARE brownie mix as directed on package. Spread batter evenly in greased 12-inch pizza pan. Bake 20 minutes. Cool completely on wire rack.

MIX cream cheese, sugar and peanut butter with electric mixer on medium speed until well blended. Spread over brownie. Arrange banana slices over cream cheese mixture; sprinkle with peanuts.

MELT chocolate and butter in heavy saucepan on very low heat, stirring constantly until just melted. Drizzle over bananas and peanuts. *Makes 12 servings*

MARBLED
PEANUT BUTTER BROWNIES

½ **cup butter, softened**
¼ **cup peanut butter**
1 **cup packed light brown sugar**
½ **cup granulated sugar**
3 **eggs**
1 **teaspoon vanilla**
2 **cups all-purpose flour**
2 **teaspoons baking powder**
⅛ **teaspoon salt**
1 **cup chocolate-flavored syrup**
½ **cup salted mixed nuts, coarsely chopped**

Preheat oven to 350°F. Lightly grease 13×9-inch pan.

Cream butter and peanut butter in large bowl until blended; stir in sugars. Beat in eggs, one at a time, until batter is light. Blend in

vanilla. Combine flour, baking powder and salt in small bowl. Stir into butter mixture.

Spread half of the batter evenly in prepared pan. Spread syrup over the top. Spoon remaining batter over syrup. Swirl with knife or spatula to create a marbled effect. Sprinkle chopped nuts over the top.

Bake 35 to 40 minutes or until lightly browned. Cool in pan on wire rack. Cut into 2-inch squares. *Makes about 2 dozen brownies*

STRAWBERRY CHOCOLATE CHIP SHORTCAKE

1 cup sugar, divided

½ cup (1 stick) butter or margarine, softened

1 egg

2 teaspoons vanilla extract, divided

1½ cups all-purpose flour

½ teaspoon baking powder

1 cup HERSHEY'S MINICHIPS™ Semi-Sweet Chocolate or HERSHEY'S Semi-Sweet Chocolate Chips, divided

2 cups (16 ounces) dairy sour cream

2 eggs

2 cups frozen non-dairy whipped topping, thawed

Fresh strawberries, rinsed and halved

Heat oven to 350°F. Grease 9-inch springform pan. In large bowl, beat ½ cup sugar and butter. Add 1 egg and 1 teaspoon vanilla; beat until creamy. Gradually add flour and baking powder, beating until smooth; stir in ½ cup small chocolate chips. Press mixture onto bottom of prepared pan. In medium bowl, stir together sour cream, remaining ½ cup sugar, 2 eggs and remaining 1 teaspoon vanilla; stir in remaining ½ cup small chocolate chips. Pour over mixture in pan. Bake 50 to 55 minutes until almost set in center and edges are lightly browned. Cool completely on wire rack; remove side of pan. Spread whipped topping over top. Cover; refrigerate. Just before serving, arrange strawberry halves on top of cake; garnish as desired. Refrigerate leftover dessert.

Makes 12 servings

FESTIVE FRUITED WHITE CHIP BLONDIES

- ½ **cup (1 stick) butter or margarine**
- 1⅔ **cups (10-ounce package) HERSHEY'S Premier White Chips, divided**
- 2 **eggs**
- ¼ **cup granulated sugar**
- 1¼ **cups all-purpose flour**
- ⅓ **cup orange juice**
- ¾ **cup cranberries, chopped**
- ¼ **cup chopped dried apricots**
- ½ **cup coarsely chopped nuts**
- ¼ **cup packed light brown sugar**

1. Heat oven to 325°F. Grease and flour 9-inch square baking pan.

2. In medium saucepan, melt butter; stir in 1 cup white chips. In large bowl, beat eggs until foamy. Add granulated sugar; beat until thick and pale yellow in color. Add flour, orange juice and white chip mixture; beat just until combined. Spread one-half of batter, about 1¼ cups, into prepared pan.

3. Bake 15 minutes until edges are lightly browned; remove from oven.

4. Stir cranberries, apricots and remaining ⅔ cup white chips into remaining one-half of batter; spread over top of hot baked mixture. Stir together nuts and brown sugar; sprinkle over top.

5. Bake 25 to 30 minutes or until edges are lightly browned. Cool completely in pan on wire rack. Cut into bars.

Makes about 16 bars

CHOCOLATE PECAN PIE

1 package (4 ounces) BAKER'S®
   GERMAN'S Sweet Chocolate
2 tablespoons margarine or butter
1 cup corn syrup
⅓ cup sugar
3 eggs
1 teaspoon vanilla
1½ cups pecan halves
1 unbaked 9-inch pie shell
   COOL WHIP® Whipped Topping,
   thawed (optional)

HEAT oven to 350°F.

MICROWAVE chocolate and margarine in large microwavable bowl on HIGH 2 minutes or until margarine is melted. Stir until chocolate is completely melted.

STIR in corn syrup, sugar, eggs and vanilla until well blended. Stir in pecans, reserving 8 halves for garnish, if desired. Pour filling into pie shell.

BAKE for 55 minutes or until knife inserted 1 inch from center comes out clean. Cool on wire rack. Garnish with whipped topping and chocolate-dipped pecan halves, if desired.

Makes 8 servings

TRIPLE CHOCOLATE BROWNIES

3 squares (1 ounce each) unsweetened chocolate, coarsely chopped

2 squares (1 ounce each) semisweet chocolate, coarsely chopped

½ cup butter

1 cup all-purpose flour

½ teaspoon salt

¼ teaspoon baking powder

1½ cups sugar

3 large eggs

1 teaspoon vanilla

¼ cup sour cream

½ cup milk chocolate chips

Powdered sugar (optional)

PREHEAT oven to 350°F. Lightly grease 13×9-inch baking pan.

PLACE unsweetened chocolate, semisweet chocolate and butter in medium microwavable bowl. Microwave at HIGH 2 minutes or until butter is melted; stir until chocolate is completely melted. Cool to room temperature.

PLACE flour, salt and baking powder in small bowl; stir to combine.

BEAT sugar, eggs and vanilla in large bowl with electric mixer at medium speed until slightly thickened. Beat in chocolate mixture until well combined. Add flour mixture; beat at low speed until blended. Add sour cream; beat at low speed until combined. Stir in milk chocolate chips. Spread mixture evenly into prepared pan.

BAKE 20 to 25 minutes or until wooden pick inserted into center comes out almost clean. (Do not overbake.) Cool brownies completely in pan on wire rack. Cut into 2-inch squares. Place powdered sugar in fine-mesh strainer; sprinkle over brownies, if desired.   *Makes 2 dozen brownies*

To-Die-For Pies

Hershey's Cocoa Cream Pie (page 97)

CARAMEL-LAYERED BROWNIES

4 squares BAKER'S® Unsweetened Chocolate
¾ cup (1½ sticks) margarine or butter
2 cups sugar
3 eggs
1 teaspoon vanilla
1 cup all-purpose flour
1 cup BAKER'S® Semi-Sweet Real Chocolate Chips
1½ cups chopped nuts, divided
1 (14-ounce) package caramels
⅓ cup evaporated milk

HEAT oven to 350°F.

MICROWAVE chocolate and margarine in large microwavable bowl on HIGH 2 minutes or until margarine is melted. Stir until chocolate is completely melted.

STIR sugar into melted chocolate mixture. Mix in eggs and vanilla until well blended. Stir in flour. Remove 1 cup of batter; set aside. Spread remaining batter into greased 13×9-inch pan. Sprinkle with chips and 1 cup of the nuts.

MICROWAVE caramels and milk in same bowl on HIGH 4 minutes, stirring after 2 minutes. Stir until caramels are completely melted and smooth. Spoon over chips and nuts, spreading to edges of pan. Gently spread reserved batter over caramel mixture. Sprinkle with the remaining ½ cup nuts.

BAKE for 40 minutes or until toothpick inserted into center comes out with fudgy crumbs. Do not overbake. Cool in pan; cut into squares.

Makes about 24 brownies

PHILLY 3-STEP™ TOFFEE CRUNCH CHEESECAKE

- 2 (8-ounce) packages **PHILADELPHIA BRAND® Cream Cheese, softened**
- ½ **cup sugar**
- ½ **teaspoon vanilla**
- 2 **eggs**
- 1 **ready-to-use graham cracker pie crust (6 ounces or 9 inches)**
- 4 **(1.4-ounce) bars chocolate-covered English toffee, chopped (1 cup)**

almost set. Cool. Refrigerate 3 hours or overnight.   *Makes 8 servings*

Cook's Notes:

For Peanut Butter Caramel Nut Cheesecake, omit toffee. Beat ⅓ cup peanut butter in with cream cheese. Sprinkle with 1 cup chopped milk chocolate with nuts and caramel candy bars (three 2.07-ounce bars) before baking.

1. MIX cream cheese, sugar and vanilla at medium speed with electric mixer until well blended. Add eggs; mix until blended.

2. POUR into crust. Sprinkle with toffee.

3. BAKE at 350°F, 40 minutes or until center is

DECADENT BLONDE BROWNIES

1½ cups all-purpose flour
1 teaspoon baking powder
½ teaspoon salt
½ cup butter, softened
¾ cup granulated sugar
¾ cup packed light brown sugar
2 large eggs
2 teaspoons vanilla
1 package (10 ounces) semisweet chocolate chunks*
1 jar (3½ ounces) macadamia nuts, coarsely chopped

*Or, cut 10-ounce thick chocolate candy bar into ½-inch pieces to equal 1½ cups.

Preheat oven to 350°F. Grease 13×9-inch baking pan. Combine flour, baking powder and salt in small bowl; set aside.

Beat butter and sugars in large bowl with electric mixer at medium speed until light and fluffy. Beat in eggs and vanilla. Add flour mixture. Beat at low speed until well blended. Stir in chocolate and nuts. Spread batter evenly into prepared baking pan. Bake 25 to 30 minutes or until golden brown. Remove pan to wire rack; cool completely. Cut into 3¼×1½-inch bars.   *Makes 2 dozen brownies*

EASY EASEL RECIPES

JEWELED BROWNIE CHEESECAKE

¾ cup (1½ sticks) butter or margarine
4 squares (1 ounce each) unsweetened baking chocolate
1½ cups sugar
4 large eggs, divided
1 cup all-purpose flour
1¾ cups "M&M's"® Chocolate Mini Baking Bits, divided
½ cup chopped walnuts (optional)
1 (8-ounce) package cream cheese, softened
1 teaspoon vanilla extract

Preheat oven to 350°F. Lightly grease 9-inch springform pan; set aside. Place butter and chocolate in large microwave-safe bowl. Microwave at HIGH 1 minute; stir. Microwave at HIGH an additional 30 seconds; stir until chocolate is completely melted. Add

sugar and 3 eggs, one at a time, beating well after each addition; blend in flour. Stir in 1¼ cups "M&M's"® Chocolate Mini Baking Bits and nuts, if desired; set aside. In large bowl, beat cream cheese, remaining 1 egg and vanilla. Spread half of the chocolate mixture in prepared pan. Carefully spread cream cheese mixture evenly over chocolate mixture, leaving 1-inch border. Spread remaining chocolate mixture evenly over top, all the way to the edges. Sprinkle with remaining ½ cup "M&M's"® Chocolate Mini Baking Bits. Bake 40 to 45 minutes or until firm to the touch. Cool completely. Store in refrigerator in tightly covered container.

Makes 12 slices

EASY EASEL
RECIPES

MINTED CHOCOLATE CHIP BROWNIES

¾ cup granulated sugar

½ cup butter

2 tablespoons water

1 cup semisweet chocolate chips or mini semisweet chocolate chips

1½ teaspoons vanilla

2 eggs

1¼ cups all-purpose flour

½ teaspoon baking soda

½ teaspoon salt

1 cup mint chocolate chips

Powdered sugar for garnish

Preheat oven to 350°F. Grease 9-inch square baking pan.

Combine sugar, butter and water in medium microwavable bowl.

Microwave on HIGH 2½ to 3 minutes or until butter is melted. Stir in semisweet chips; stir gently until chips are melted and mixture is well blended. Stir in vanilla; let stand 5 minutes to cool.

Beat eggs into chocolate mixture, 1 at a time. Combine flour, baking soda and salt in small bowl; add to chocolate mixture. Stir in mint chocolate chips. Spread into prepared pan.

Bake 25 or 30 minutes. Remove pan to wire rack; cool completely. Cut into squares. Sprinkle with powdered sugar, if desired.

Makes about 16 brownies

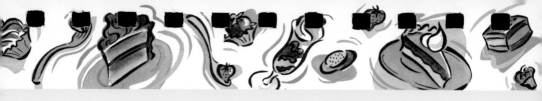

BROWNIE BOTTOM CHEESECAKE

½ cup (1 stick) butter

4 squares BAKER'S® Unsweetened Chocolate

2¼ cups sugar, divided

2 eggs

¼ cup milk

2 teaspoons vanilla, divided

1 cup flour

½ teaspoon salt

3 (8-ounce) packages PHILADELPHIA BRAND® Cream Cheese, softened

3 eggs

½ cup sour cream

MELT butter and chocolate in 3-quart heavy saucepan over low heat, stirring constantly; cool. Blend in 1½ cups of the sugar.

ADD 2 eggs, 1 at a time, mixing on low speed after each addition until blended. Blend in milk and 1 teaspoon vanilla. Mix flour and salt. Add to chocolate mixture, mixing just until blended. Spread evenly onto bottom of greased and floured 9-inch springform pan. Bake at 325°F for 25 minutes.

MIX cream cheese, remaining ¾ cup sugar and 1 teaspoon vanilla with electric mixer on medium speed until well blended. Add remaining 3 eggs, 1 at a time, mixing on low speed after each addition, just until blended. Blend in sour cream; pour over brownie bottom (filling will almost come to top of pan).

BAKE at 325°F for 55 minutes to 1 hour or until center is almost set. Run knife or metal spatula around rim of pan to loosen cake; cool before removing rim of pan. Refrigerate 4 hours or overnight. Let stand at room temperature 30 minutes before serving. Drizzle with assorted ice cream toppings, if desired. *Makes 12 servings*

ORANGE CAPPUCCINO BROWNIES

¾ **cup butter**

2 **squares (1 ounce each) semisweet chocolate, coarsely chopped**

2 **squares (1 ounce each) unsweetened chocolate, coarsely chopped**

1¾ **cups granulated sugar**

1 **tablespoon instant espresso powder**

3 **eggs**

¼ **cup orange-flavored liqueur**

2 **teaspoons grated orange peel**

1 **cup all-purpose flour**

1 **package (12 ounces) semisweet chocolate chips**

2 **tablespoons shortening**

Preheat oven to 350°F. Grease 13×9-inch baking pan.

Melt butter and chopped chocolates in large

saucepan over low heat, stirring constantly. Stir in granulated sugar and espresso powder. Remove from heat. Cool slightly. Beat in eggs, 1 at a time, with wire whisk. Whisk in liqueur and orange peel. Beat flour into chocolate mixture until just blended. Spread batter in prepared pan.

Bake 25 to 30 minutes or until center is just set. Remove pan to wire rack. Meanwhile, melt chocolate chips and shortening in small saucepan over low heat, stirring constantly. Immediately, spread chocolate mixture over warm brownies. Cool completely on wire rack. Cut into 2-inch squares.

Makes about 2 dozen brownies

PHILLY 3-STEP™ CHOCOLATE CHIP COOKIE DOUGH CHEESECAKE

2 (8-ounce) packages PHILADELPHIA
  BRAND® Cream Cheese, softened
½ cup sugar
½ teaspoon vanilla
2 eggs
¾ cup prepared chocolate chip cookie
  dough, divided
1 ready-to-use graham cracker pie crust
  (6 ounces or 9 inches)

1. MIX cream cheese, sugar and vanilla at medium speed with electric mixer until well blended. Add eggs; mix until blended. Drop ½ cup of the cookie dough by level teaspoonfuls into batter; fold gently.

2. POUR into crust. Dot with level teaspoonfuls of remaining ¼ cup cookie dough.

3. BAKE at 350°F, 40 minutes or until center is almost set. Cool. Refrigerate 3 hours or overnight.   *Makes 8 servings*

EASY EASEL RECIPES

DOUBLE-DECKER CONFETTI BROWNIES

- ¾ cup (1½ sticks) butter or margarine, softened
- 1 cup granulated sugar
- 1 cup firmly packed light brown sugar
- 3 large eggs
- 1 teaspoon vanilla extract
- 2½ cups all-purpose flour, divided
- 2½ teaspoons baking powder
- ½ teaspoon salt
- ⅓ cup unsweetened cocoa powder
- 1 tablespoon butter or margarine, melted
- 1 cup "M&M's"® Semi-Sweet Chocolate Mini Baking Bits, divided

Preheat oven to 350°F. Lightly grease 13×9×2-inch baking pan; set

aside. In large bowl, cream butter and sugars until light and fluffy; beat in eggs and vanilla. In medium bowl, combine 2¼ cups flour, baking powder and salt; blend into creamed mixture. Divide batter in half. Blend together cocoa powder and melted butter; stir into one half of the dough. Spread cocoa dough evenly into prepared baking pan. Stir remaining ¼ cup flour and ½ cup "M&M's"® Semi-Sweet Chocolate Mini Baking Bits into remaining dough; spread evenly over cocoa dough in pan. Sprinkle with remaining ½ cup baking bits. Bake 25 to 30 minutes or until edges start to pull away from sides of pan. Cool completely. Cut into bars.

Makes 24 brownies

FUDGE TRUFFLE CHEESECAKE

Chocolate Crumb Crust (recipe follows)

2 cups (12-ounce package) HERSHEY'S Semi-Sweet Chocolate Chips

3 packages (8 ounces each) cream cheese, softened

1 can (14 ounces) sweetened condensed milk

4 eggs

¼ cup coffee-flavored liqueur (optional)

2 teaspoons vanilla extract

Heat oven to 300°F. Prepare Chocolate Crumb Crust. In microwave-safe bowl, place chocolate chips. Microwave at HIGH (100%) 1½ to 2 minutes or until chocolate is melted and smooth when stirred. In large mixer bowl, beat cream cheese until fluffy. Gradually beat in

sweetened condensed milk until smooth. Add melted chocolate and remaining ingredients; mix well. Pour into prepared Chocolate Crumb Crust. Bake 1 hour and 5 minutes or until center is set. Remove from oven to wire rack. With knife, loosen cake from side of pan. Cool completely; remove side of pan. Refrigerate before serving.

Makes 10 to 12 servings

Chocolate Crumb Crust: In medium bowl, stir together 1½ cups vanilla wafer crumbs, ½ cup powdered sugar, ⅓ cup HERSHEY'S Cocoa and ⅓ cup melted butter or margarine. Press firmly on bottom of 9-inch springform pan.

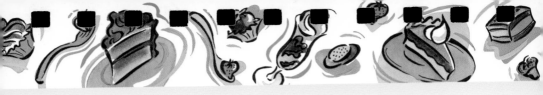

ROCKY ROAD BROWNIES

½ **cup butter**
½ **cup unsweetened cocoa**
1 **cup sugar**
1 **egg**
½ **cup all-purpose flour**
¼ **cup buttermilk**
1 **teaspoon vanilla**
1 **cup miniature marshmallows**
1 **cup coarsely chopped walnuts**
1 **cup (6 ounces) semisweet chocolate chips**

Preheat oven to 350°F. Lightly grease an 8-inch square pan.

Combine butter and cocoa in medium saucepan over low heat, stirring constantly until smooth. Remove from heat; stir in sugar, egg, flour, buttermilk and vanilla.

Mix until smooth. Spread batter evenly in prepared pan. Bake 25 minutes or until center feels dry. (Do not overbake or brownies will be dry.) Remove from oven; sprinkle marshmallows, walnuts and chocolate chips over the top. Return to oven for 3 to 5 minutes or just until topping is warmed enough to meld together. Cool in pan on wire rack. Cut into 2-inch squares.

Makes 16 brownies

Cook's Notes:
Walnuts can be chopped quickly and easily in the food processor. Use brief on/off pulses and be careful not to overprocess.

WHITE CHOCOLATE CHEESECAKE

CRUST

- ½ **cup (1 stick) butter**
- ¼ **cup sugar**
- ½ **teaspoon vanilla**
- 1 **cup all-purpose flour**

FILLING

- 4 **(8-ounce) packages PHILADELPHIA BRAND® Cream Cheese, softened**
- ½ **cup sugar**
- 1 **teaspoon vanilla**
- 4 **eggs**
- 12 **ounces white chocolate, melted, slightly cooled**

• **HEAT** oven to 325°F.

• **CREAM** butter, sugar and vanilla in small bowl at medium speed with electric mixer until light and fluffy. Gradually add flour, mixing at low speed

until blended. Press onto bottom of 9-inch springform pan; prick with fork.

• **BAKE** 25 minutes or until edges are light golden brown.

• **BEAT** cream cheese, sugar and vanilla at medium speed with electric mixer until well blended. Add eggs, 1 at a time, mixing at low speed after each addition, just until blended.

• **BLEND** in melted chocolate; pour over crust.

• **BAKE** 55 to 60 minutes or until center is almost set. Run knife or metal spatula around rim of pan to loosen cake; cool before removing rim of pan. Refrigerate 4 hours or overnight. Garnish with chocolate curls and powdered sugar.

Makes 12 servings

RASPBERRY FUDGE BROWNIES

½ **cup butter**

3 **squares (1 ounce each) bittersweet chocolate**

2 **eggs**

1 **cup sugar**

1 **teaspoon vanilla**

¾ **cup all-purpose flour**

¼ **teaspoon baking powder**
 Dash salt

½ **cup sliced or slivered almonds**

½ **cup raspberry preserves**

1 **cup (6 ounces) milk chocolate chips**

Preheat oven to 350°F. Grease and flour 8-inch square baking pan.

Melt butter and bittersweet chocolate in small saucepan over low heat, stirring constantly. Remove from heat; cool. Beat eggs, sugar and vanilla in large bowl until light. Beat in

chocolate mixture. Stir in flour, baking powder and salt until just blended. Spread ¾ of batter in prepared pan; sprinkle almonds over top.

Bake 10 minutes. Remove from oven; spread preserves over almonds. Carefully spoon remaining batter over preserves, smoothing top. Bake 25 to 30 minutes or just until top feels firm.

Remove from oven; sprinkle chocolate chips over top. Let stand a few minutes until chips melt, then spread evenly over brownies. Cool completely in pan on wire rack. When chocolate is set, cut into 2-inch squares.

Makes 16 brownies

CHOCOLATE TURTLE CHEESECAKE

24 chocolate sandwich cookies, ground
   (about 2¾ cups)
 2 tablespoons butter, melted
 2 packages (8 ounces each) cream
   cheese, softened
 ⅓ cup sugar
 ¼ cup sour cream
 2 eggs
 1 teaspoon vanilla
 ½ cup prepared caramel sauce
 ½ cup prepared fudge sauce
 ½ cup pecan halves

1. Preheat oven to 350°F.
Combine ground cookies
and butter in medium
bowl; pat evenly on
bottom and 1 inch up side
of 9-inch springform pan.
Place in freezer while
preparing filling.

2. Beat cream cheese in
large bowl with electric

mixer until fluffy. Beat in sugar, sour cream,
eggs and vanilla until smooth. Pour mixture
into prepared crust.

3. Bake cheesecake 30 to 35 minutes or
until almost set in center. Cool on wire rack.
Refrigerate, loosely covered, 8 hours or up to
3 days.

4. Remove side of springform pan from
cheesecake; place on serving plate. Drizzle
caramel and fudge sauces over cake; cut cake
into wedges. Top each
serving with 2 to 3 pecan
halves.

Makes 12 servings

EASY EASEL
RECIPES

THREE GREAT TASTES BLOND BROWNIES

2 cups packed light brown sugar

1 cup (2 sticks) butter or margarine, melted

2 eggs

2 teaspoons vanilla extract

2 cups all-purpose flour

1 teaspoon salt

⅔ cup (of each) HERSHEY'S Semi-Sweet Chocolate Chips, REESE'S® Peanut Butter Chips, and HERSHEY'S Premier White Chips

Chocolate Chip Drizzle (recipe follows)

1. Heat oven to 350°F. Grease 15½×10½×1-inch jelly-roll pan.

2. In large bowl, stir together brown sugar and butter; beat in eggs and vanilla until smooth. Add flour and salt, beating just until blended; stir in chocolate, peanut butter and white chips. Spread batter into prepared pan.

3. Bake 25 to 30 minutes or until wooden pick inserted in center comes out clean. Cool completely in pan on wire rack. Cut into bars. With tines of fork, drizzle CHOCOLATE CHIP DRIZZLE randomly over bars.

Makes about 72 bars

Chocolate Chip Drizzle: In small microwave-safe bowl, place ¼ cup HERSHEY'S Semi-Sweet Chocolate Chips and ¼ teaspoon shortening (do not use butter, margarine or oil). Microwave at HIGH (100%) 30 seconds to 1 minute; stir until chips are melted and mixture is smooth.

COOKIES AND CREAM CHEESECAKE

CRUST

- 1 **cup finely crushed chocolate sandwich cookies**
- 1 **tablespoon PARKAY® Spread Sticks, melted**

FILLING

- 3 **(8 ounce) packages PHILADELPHIA BRAND® Cream Cheese, softened**
- 1 **cup sugar**
- 2 **tablespoons flour**
- 1 **teaspoon vanilla**
- 3 **eggs**
- 1 **cup coarsely chopped chocolate sandwich cookies**

• **HEAT** oven to 325°F.

CRUST

• **MIX** crumbs and PARKAY spread; press onto bottom of 9-inch springform pan. Bake 10 minutes.

FILLING

• **BEAT** cream cheese, sugar, flour and vanilla at medium speed with electric mixer until well blended. Add eggs, 1 at a time, mixing at low speed after each addition, just until blended.

• **FOLD** in chopped cookies; pour over crust.

• **BAKE** 1 hour and 5 minutes or until center is almost set. Run knife or metal spatula around rim of pan to loosen cake; cool before removing rim of pan. Refrigerate 4 hours or overnight. Garnish with COOL WHIP Whipped Topping, chocolate sandwich cookies, cut in half, and mint leaves.

Makes 12 servings

EASY EASEL RECIPES

P.B. CHIPS BROWNIE CUPS

1 cup (2 sticks) butter or margarine
2 cups sugar
2 teaspoons vanilla extract
4 eggs
¾ cup HERSHEY'S Cocoa or HERSHEY'S Dutch Processed Cocoa
1¾ cups all-purpose flour
½ teaspoon baking powder
½ teaspoon salt
1⅔ cups (10-ounce package) REESE'S Peanut Butter Chips, divided

1. Heat oven to 350°F. Line 18 muffin cups (2½ inches in diameter) with paper or foil bake cups.

2. In large microwave-safe bowl, place butter. Microwave at HIGH (100%) 1 to 1½ minutes or until melted. Stir in sugar and vanilla. Add eggs; beat well. Add cocoa; beat until well blended. Add flour, baking powder and salt; beat well. Stir in 1⅓ cups peanut butter chips. Divide batter evenly into muffin cups; sprinkle with remaining ⅓ cup peanut butter chips.

3. Bake 25 to 30 minutes or until surface is firm; cool completely in pan on wire rack.

Makes about 1½ dozen brownie cups

Cook's Notes:
Hershey's Dutch Processed Cocoa involves a process which neutralizes the natural acidity found in cocoa powder. This results in a darker cocoa with a more mellow flavor than natural cocoa.

EASY EASEL RECIPES

EASY CHOCOLATE CHEESECAKE

1¾ cups chocolate cookie or graham
     cracker crumbs

2 tablespoons sugar

⅓ cup margarine or butter, melted

2 packages (4 ounces each) BAKER'S®
     GERMAN'S® Sweet Chocolate,
     divided

2 eggs

⅔ cup light or dark corn syrup

⅓ cup heavy cream

1½ teaspoons vanilla

2 packages (8 ounces each)
     PHILADELPHIA
     BRAND® Cream
     Cheese, cut into
     cubes and softened

HEAT oven to 325°F.

COMBINE cookie crumbs,
sugar and margarine in
9-inch pie plate or
springform pan until well
mixed. Press into pie plate

or onto bottom and 1¼ inches up sides of
springform pan.

MICROWAVE 1½ packages (6 ounces)
chocolate in microwavable bowl on HIGH
1½ to 2 minutes, stirring halfway through
heating time. Stir until completely melted.
Place eggs, corn syrup, cream and vanilla in
blender container; cover. Blend until smooth.
With blender running, gradually add cream
cheese, blending until smooth. Blend in
melted chocolate. Pour into crust.

BAKE 50 to 55 minutes or
until center is almost set.
Cool on wire rack. Cover;
refrigerate 3 hours or
overnight. Just before
serving, melt remaining ½
package (2 ounces)
chocolate and drizzle over
top.　　*Makes 8 servings*

SENSATIONAL PEPPERMINT PATTIE BROWNIES

24 small (1½-inch) YORK® Peppermint Patties

1½ cups (3 sticks) butter or margarine, melted

3 cups sugar

1 tablespoon vanilla extract

5 eggs

2 cups all-purpose flour

1 cup HERSHEY'S Cocoa

1 teaspoon baking powder

1 teaspoon salt

Heat oven to 350°F. Remove wrappers from peppermint patties. Grease 13×9×2-inch baking pan.

In large bowl, stir together butter, sugar and vanilla. Add eggs; beat until well blended. Stir together flour, cocoa, baking powder and

salt; gradually add to butter mixture, blending well. Reserve 2 cups batter. Spread remaining batter into prepared pan. Arrange peppermint patties about ½ inch apart in single layer over batter. Spread reserved batter over patties.

Bake 50 to 55 minutes or until brownies pull away from sides of pan. Cool completely in pan on wire rack.

Makes 36 brownies

EASY EASEL RECIPES

Sinful Cheesecakes

Brownie Bottom Cheesecake (page 86)

WHITE CHOCOLATE CHUNK BROWNIES

4 squares (1 ounce each) unsweetened chocolate, coarsely chopped
½ cup butter
2 large eggs
1¼ cups sugar
1 teaspoon vanilla
½ cup all-purpose flour
½ teaspoon salt
6 ounces white baking bar, cut into ¼-inch pieces
½ cup coarsely chopped walnuts
Powdered sugar

Preheat oven to 350°F. Grease 8-inch square baking pan; set aside.

Melt unsweetened chocolate and butter in small saucepan over low heat, stirring constantly; set aside.

Beat eggs in large bowl with electric mixer at medium speed 30 seconds. Gradually add sugar, beating at medium speed about 4 minutes until very thick and lemon colored.

Beat in chocolate mixture and vanilla. Beat in flour and salt at low speed just until blended. Stir in baking bar pieces and walnuts. Spread batter evenly into prepared baking pan.

Bake 30 minutes or until edges just begin to pull away from sides of pan and center is set.

Remove pan to wire rack; cool completely. Cut into 2-inch squares. Sprinkle powdered sugar over brownies.

Makes 16 brownies

CHOCOLATE DREAM TORTE

1 **package DUNCAN HINES® Moist Deluxe® Dark Chocolate Cake Mix**

1 **package (6 ounces) semi-sweet chocolate chips, melted, for garnish**

1 **container (8 ounces) frozen whipped topping, thawed and divided**

1 **container (16 ounces) DUNCAN HINES® Creamy Homestyle Milk Chocolate Frosting**

3 **tablespoons finely chopped dry roasted pistachios**

1. Preheat oven to 350°F. Grease and flour two 9-inch round cake pans.

2. Prepare, bake and cool cake following package directions for basic recipe.

3. For chocolate hearts garnish, spread melted chocolate to ⅛-inch thickness on waxed-

paper-lined baking sheet. Cut shapes with heart cookie cutter when chocolate begins to set. Refrigerate until firm. Push out heart shapes. Set aside.

4. To assemble, split each cake layer in half horizontally. Place one split cake layer on serving plate. Spread one-third of whipped topping on top. Repeat with remaining layers and whipped topping, leaving top plain. Frost sides and top with Milk Chocolate frosting. Sprinkle pistachios on top. Position chocolate hearts by pushing points down into cake. Refrigerate until ready to serve.

Makes 12 servings

BUTTERSCOTCH BROWNIES

1 cup butterscotch-flavored chips
¼ cup butter, softened
½ cup packed light brown sugar
2 eggs
½ teaspoon vanilla
1 cup all-purpose flour
½ teaspoon baking powder
¼ teaspoon salt
1 cup semisweet chocolate chips

Preheat oven to 350°F. Grease 9-inch square baking pan.

Melt butterscotch chips in small saucepan over low heat stirring constantly; set aside.

Beat butter and sugar in large bowl until light and fluffy. Beat in eggs, 1 at a time. Beat in vanilla and melted butterscotch chips. Combine flour,

baking powder and salt in small bowl; add to butter mixture. Beat until well blended. Spread batter evenly in prepared pan.

Bake 20 to 25 minutes or until golden brown and center is set. Remove pan from oven and immediately sprinkle with chocolate chips. Let stand about 4 minutes or until chocolate is melted. Spread chocolate evenly over top. Place pan on wire rack; cool completely. Cut into 2¼-inch squares.

Makes about 16 brownies

STRAWBERRY CHOCOLATE ROLL

3 large eggs, separated
½ cup sugar
5 ounces semisweet chocolate, melted
⅓ cup water
1 teaspoon vanilla
¾ cup all-purpose flour
1 teaspoon baking powder
½ teaspoon baking soda
¼ teaspoon salt
　Unsweetened cocoa
½ cup seedless strawberry jam
2 pints strawberry ice cream, softened

Preheat oven to 350°F. Line 15×10-inch jelly-roll pan with foil, extending foil 1 inch over ends of pan. Grease and flour foil.

Beat egg yolks and sugar in medium bowl until light and fluffy. Beat in melted chocolate. Add water and vanilla. Mix until smooth. Sift flour, baking powder, baking soda and salt together. Add to chocolate mixture.

Beat egg whites in large bowl with electric mixer until soft peaks form. Gently fold in chocolate mixture. Pour into prepared pan.

Bake 8 to 9 minutes or until wooden pick inserted into center comes out clean. Carefully loosen sides of cake from foil. Invert cake onto towel sprinkled with cocoa. Peel off foil. Starting at short end, roll warm cake, jelly-roll fashion with towel inside. Cool cake completely.

Unroll cake and remove towel. Spread cake with jam. Spread ice cream, leaving a ¼-inch border. Roll up cake. Wrap tightly in plastic wrap or foil. Freeze until firm. Allow cake to stand at room temperature 10 minutes before cutting and serving.

Makes 8 to 12 servings

Best-Ever Bars

Rich Chocolate Chip Toffee Bars (page 56)

PUDDING POKE CAKE

1 **package (2-layer size) chocolate cake mix or cake mix with pudding in the mix**
4 **cups cold milk**
2 **packages (4-serving size) JELL-O® Vanilla Flavor Instant Pudding & Pie Filling**

PREPARE and bake cake mix as directed on package for 13×9-inch baking pan. Remove from oven. Immediately poke holes down through cake to pan at 1-inch intervals with round handle of a wooden spoon. (Or poke holes with a plastic drinking straw, using turning motion to make large holes.)

POUR milk into large bowl. Add pudding mixes. Beat with wire whisk 2 minutes. Quickly pour about ½ of the thin pudding mixture evenly over warm cake and

into holes. Let remaining pudding mixture stand to thicken slightly. Spoon over top of cake, swirling to frost cake.

REFRIGERATE at least 1 hour or until ready to serve. *Makes 15 servings*

· ·

Cook's Notes:

This cake is a real kid-pleaser. Let them help you out in the kitchen by poking the holes in the cake and mixing the pudding.

· ·

EASY EASEL RECIPES

DOUBLE CHOCOLATE FANTASY BARS

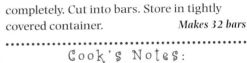

2 cups chocolate cookie crumbs
⅓ cup (5⅓ tablespoons) butter or margarine, melted
1 14-ounce can sweetened condensed milk
1¾ cups "M&M's"® Semi-Sweet Chocolate Mini Baking Bits
1 cup shredded coconut
1 cup chopped walnuts or pecans

Preheat oven to 350°F.

In large bowl combine cookie crumbs and butter; press mixture onto bottom of 13×9×2-inch baking pan. Pour condensed milk evenly over crumbs. Combine "M&M's"® Semi-Sweet Chocolate Mini Baking Bits, coconut and nuts. Sprinkle mixture evenly over condensed milk; press down lightly.

Bake 25 to 30 minutes or until set. Cool completely. Cut into bars. Store in tightly covered container.   *Makes 32 bars*

....

Cook's Notes:

Sweetened condensed milk is a mixture of milk and sugar heated until about half of the liquid evaporates. Sweetened condensed milk is available in cans and should not be confused with evaporated milk, which has no sugar added.

....

CHOCOLATE CHERRY TORTE

1 package DUNCAN HINES® Moist
    Deluxe® Devil's Food Cake Mix
1 can (21 ounces) cherry pie filling
¼ teaspoon almond extract
1 container (8 ounces) frozen whipped
    topping, thawed and divided
¼ cup toasted sliced almonds, for
    garnish

1. Preheat oven to 350°F. Grease and flour
two 9-inch round cake pans.

2. Prepare, bake and cool
cake following package
directions for basic recipe.
Combine cherry pie filling
and almond extract in
small bowl. Stir until
blended.

3. To assemble, place one
cake layer on serving
plate. Spread with 1 cup
whipped topping, then

half the cherry pie filling mixture. Top with
second cake layer. Spread remaining pie
filling to within 1½ inches of cake edge.
Decorate cake edge with remaining whipped
topping. Garnish with sliced almonds.

Makes 12 to 16 servings

Cook's Notes:

*To toast almonds, spread in a single layer
on baking sheet. Bake at 325°F 4 to 6 minutes
or until fragrant and golden.*

CHOCO CHEESECAKE SQUARES

⅓ cup butter, softened
⅓ cup packed light brown sugar
1 cup plus 1 tablespoon all-purpose
  flour, divided
½ cup chopped pecans (optional)
1 cup semisweet chocolate chips
1 package (8 ounces) cream cheese,
  softened
¼ cup granulated sugar
1 large egg
1 teaspoon vanilla

Preheat oven to 350°F. Grease 8-inch square baking pan; set aside.

Beat butter and brown sugar in large bowl until light and fluffy. Add 1 cup flour. Beat until well combined. Stir in nuts, if desired. (Mixture will be crumbly.)

Press evenly into prepared pan. Bake 15 minutes.

Melt chocolate chips in small saucepan over low heat, stirring constantly. Beat cream cheese and granulated sugar in medium bowl until light and fluffy. Add remaining 1 tablespoon flour, egg and vanilla; beat until smooth. Gradually stir in melted chocolate, mixing well. Pour cream cheese mixture over partially baked crust. Return to oven; bake 15 minutes or until set. Remove pan to wire rack; cool completely. Cut into 2-inch squares.

Makes about 16 squares

CRUNCHY-TOPPED COCOA CAKE

1½ **cups all-purpose flour**
1 **cup sugar**
¼ **cup HERSHEY'S Cocoa**
1 **teaspoon baking soda**
½ **teaspoon salt**
1 **cup water**
¼ **cup plus 2 tablespoons vegetable oil**
1 **tablespoon white vinegar**
1 **teaspoon vanilla extract**
   Broiled Topping (recipe follows)

1. Heat oven to 350°F. Grease and flour 8-inch square baking pan.

2. Stir together flour, sugar, cocoa, baking soda and salt in large bowl. Add water, oil, vinegar and vanilla; beat with spoon or whisk just until batter is smooth and ingredients are well blended. Pour batter into prepared pan.

3. Bake 35 to 40 minutes or until wooden pick inserted in center comes out clean. Meanwhile, prepare BROILED TOPPING; spread on warm cake. Set oven to broil; place pan about 4 inches from heat. Broil 3 minutes or until top is bubbly and golden brown. Remove from oven. Cool completely in pan on wire rack.   *Makes 9 servings*

Broiled Topping

¼ **cup (½ stick) butter or margarine, softened**
½ **cup packed light brown sugar**
½ **cup coarsely chopped nuts**
½ **cup MOUNDS™ Sweetened Coconut Flakes**
3 **tablespoons light cream or evaporated milk**

Stir together all ingredients in small bowl until well blended.

Makes about 1 cup topping

RICH CHOCOLATE CHIP TOFFEE BARS

2⅓ cups all-purpose flour
⅔ cup packed light brown sugar
¾ cup (1½ sticks) butter or margarine
1 egg, slightly beaten
2 cups (12-ounce package) HERSHEY'S Semi-Sweet Chocolate Chips, divided
1 cup coarsely chopped nuts
1 can (14 ounces) sweetened condensed milk (not evaporated milk)
1¾ cups (10-ounce package) SKOR® English Toffee Bits, divided

1. Heat oven to 350°F. Grease 13×9×2-inch baking pan.

2. In large bowl, stir together flour and brown sugar. Cut in butter with pastry blender until mixture resembles coarse crumbs. Add egg; mix well. Stir in 1½ cups chocolate chips and nuts. Reserve 1½ cups mixture. Press remaining crumb mixture onto bottom of prepared pan.

3. Bake 10 minutes. Pour sweetened condensed milk evenly over hot crust. Top with 1½ cups toffee bits. Sprinkle reserved crumb mixture and remaining ½ cup chips over top.

4. Bake 25 to 30 minutes or until golden brown. Sprinkle with remaining ¼ cup toffee bits. Cool completely in pan on wire rack. Cut into bars.

Makes about 36 bars

HOT FUDGE PUDDING CAKE

1 ¼ **cups granulated sugar, divided**
  1 **cup all-purpose flour**
  7 **tablespoons HERSHEY'S Cocoa, divided**
  2 **teaspoons baking powder**
  ¼ **teaspoon salt**
  ½ **cup milk**
  ⅓ **cup butter or margarine, melted**
1 ½ **teaspoons vanilla extract**
  ½ **cup packed light brown sugar**
1 ¼ **cups hot water**
    Whipped topping

Heat oven to 350°F.

In bowl, stir together ¾ cup granulated sugar, flour, 3 tablespoons cocoa, baking powder and salt. Stir in milk, butter and vanilla; beat until smooth.

Pour batter into 8- or 9-inch square baking pan. Stir together remaining ½ cup granulated sugar, brown sugar and remaining 4 tablespoons cocoa; sprinkle mixture evenly over batter. Pour hot water over top; do not stir.

Bake 35 to 40 minutes or until center is almost set. Let stand 15 minutes; spoon into dessert dishes, spooning sauce from bottom of pan over top. Garnish with whipped topping, if desired. *Makes about 8 servings*

NO-FUSS BAR COOKIES

24 graham cracker squares
1 cup semisweet chocolate chips
1 cup flaked coconut
¾ cup coarsely chopped walnuts
1 can (14 ounces) sweetened condensed milk

1. Preheat oven to 350°F. Grease 13×9-inch baking pan; set aside.

2. Place graham crackers in food processor. Process until crackers form fine crumbs. Measure 2 cups of crumbs. Combine crumbs, chips, coconut and walnuts in medium bowl; stir to blend. Add milk; stir with spoon until blended.

3. Spread batter evenly into prepared pan. Bake 15 to 18 minutes or until edges are golden brown.

4. Remove pan to wire rack; cool completely. Cut into 2¼×2¼-inch bars.   *Makes 24 bars*

Cook's Notes:
It is best to purchase nuts in small quantities, as their high fat content makes them go rancid more quickly than other dry ingredients. Store nuts in an airtight container in a cool, dry place.

EASY EASEL RECIPES

CHOCOLATE BANANA CAKE

CAKE

- 1 package **DUNCAN HINES® Moist Deluxe® Devil's Food Cake Mix**
- 3 eggs
- 1⅓ cups milk
- ½ cup **CRISCO® Vegetable Oil**

TOPPING

- 1 package (4-serving size) banana cream instant pudding and pie filling mix
- 1 cup milk
- 1 cup whipping cream, whipped
- 1 medium banana
  Lemon juice
  Chocolate sprinkles

1. Preheat oven to 350°F. Grease and flour 13×9×2-inch pan.

2. For cake, combine cake mix, eggs, milk and oil in large bowl. Beat at low speed with electric mixer until moistened. Beat at medium speed 2 minutes. Pour into pan. Bake at 350°F 35 to 38 minutes or until toothpick inserted in center comes out clean. Cool completely.

3. For topping, combine pudding mix and milk in large bowl. Stir until smooth. Fold in whipped cream. Spread on top of cooled cake. Slice banana; dip in lemon juice. Arrange on top. Garnish with chocolate sprinkles. Refrigerate until ready to serve.

Makes 12 to 16 servings

Cook's Notes:
A wire whisk is a great utensil to use when making instant pudding. It quickly eliminates all lumps.

NAOMI'S REVEL BARS

1 **cup plus 2 tablespoons butter,
    softened, divided**
2 **cups packed brown sugar**
2 **eggs**
2 **teaspoons vanilla**
2½ **cups all-purpose flour**
1 **teaspoon baking soda**
3 **cups rolled oats, uncooked**
1 **package (12 ounces) semisweet
    chocolate chips**
1 **can (14 ounces) sweetened condensed
    milk**

Preheat oven to 325°F.
Grease 13×9-inch baking
pan.

Beat 1 cup butter and
brown sugar in large
bowl. Add eggs; beat until
light and fluffy. Blend in
vanilla. Combine flour
and baking soda in
medium bowl; stir into

butter mixture. Blend in oats. Spread ¾ oat
mixture in prepared pan.

Combine chocolate chips, sweetened
condensed milk and remaining 2 tablespoons
butter in small saucepan. Stir over low heat
until chocolate is melted. Pour chocolate
mixture evenly over oat mixture in pan. Dot
with remaining oat mixture. Bake 20 to 25
minutes or until edges are browned and
center feels firm. Cool in pan on wire rack.
Cut into 2×1½-inch bars.   *Makes 36 bars*

EASY EASEL RECIPES

CHOCOLATE CHUNK COFFEE CAKE

NUT LAYER
- 1 package (4 ounces) BAKER'S® GERMAN'S Sweet Chocolate, chopped
- ½ cup chopped nuts
- ¼ cup sugar
- 1 teaspoon cinnamon

CAKE
- 1¾ cups all-purpose flour
- ½ teaspoon CALUMET® Baking Powder
- ¼ teaspoon salt
- 1 cup sour cream or plain yogurt
- 1 teaspoon baking soda
- ½ cup (1 stick) margarine or butter, softened
- 1 cup sugar
- 2 eggs
- ½ teaspoon vanilla

HEAT oven to 350°F.

MIX chocolate, nuts, ¼ cup sugar and cinnamon; set

aside. Mix flour, baking powder and salt; set aside. Combine sour cream and baking soda; set aside.

BEAT margarine and 1 cup sugar in large bowl until light and fluffy. Add eggs, one at a time, beating well after each addition. Add vanilla. Add flour mixture alternately with sour cream mixture, beginning and ending with flour mixture. Spoon ½ the batter into greased 9-inch square pan. Top with ½ the chocolate-nut mixture, spreading carefully with spatula. Repeat layers.

BAKE for 30 to 35 minutes or until cake begins to pull away from sides of pan. Cool in pan; cut into squares.

Makes 9 servings

MINI KISS COCONUT MACAROON BARS

3¾ **cups (10-ounce package) MOUNDS™**
   Sweetened Coconut Flakes
¾ **cup sugar**
¼ **cup all-purpose flour**
¼ **teaspoon salt**
3 **egg whites**
1 **whole egg, slightly beaten**
1 **teaspoon almond extract**
1 **cup HERSHEY'S MINI KISSES™**
   Chocolate

1. Heat oven to 350°F. Lightly grease 9-inch square baking pan.

2. Stir together coconut, sugar, flour and salt in large bowl. Add egg whites, whole egg and almond extract; stir until well blended.

3. Stir in MINI KISSES™. Spread mixture into prepared pan, covering all chocolate pieces with coconut mixture.

4. Bake 35 minutes or until lightly browned. Cool completely in pan on wire rack. Cover with foil; allow to stand at room temperature about 8 hours or overnight. Cut into bars.
Makes about 24 bars

ZUCCHINI CHOCOLATE CAKE

1⅔ cups granulated sugar
½ cup (1 stick) butter, softened
½ cup vegetable oil
2 eggs
1 teaspoon vanilla
½ teaspoon chocolate extract
2½ cups all-purpose flour
¼ cup cocoa
1 teaspoon baking soda
½ teaspoon salt
½ cup buttermilk
2 cups shredded
zucchini
(2 to 3 medium
zucchini)
½ cup chopped nuts
1 (6-ounce) package
semisweet
chocolate chips

Preheat oven to 325°F.
Grease and flour 13×9-
inch baking pan.

Beat together sugar, butter and oil in large bowl until well blended. Add eggs, one at a time, beating well after each addition. Blend in vanilla and chocolate extract.

Combine dry ingredients in medium bowl. Add to butter mixture alternately with buttermilk, beating well after each addition. Stir in zucchini. Pour into prepared pan. Sprinkle with nuts and chocolate chips.

Bake 55 minutes or until wooden pick inserted in center comes out clean; cool on wire rack. Cut into squares.
Makes one 13×9-inch cake

MICROWAVE CHEWY GRANOLA SQUARES

½ cup (1 stick) margarine or butter
½ cup firmly packed brown sugar
1 egg
½ teaspoon vanilla
1 cup quick oats
½ cup all-purpose flour
½ teaspoon baking soda
½ teaspoon cinnamon
¼ teaspoon salt
1 cup BAKER'S® Semi-Sweet Real Chocolate Chips, divided
½ cup raisins

BEAT margarine, sugar, egg and vanilla until light and fluffy in large bowl.

STIR in oats, flour, baking soda, cinnamon and salt. Stir in ½ cup of chips and raisins.

SPREAD into greased 8-inch square microwavable dish.

MICROWAVE on HIGH 2 minutes; rotate dish. Microwave 2 minutes longer or until toothpick inserted into center comes out clean. Sprinkle with the remaining ½ cup chips; microwave 1 minute longer. Cool in pan on countertop 15 minutes; cut into squares.   *Makes about 16 squares*

CHOCOLATE PEANUT BUTTER CUPS

1 package DUNCAN HINES® Moist Deluxe® Swiss Chocolate Cake Mix

1 container DUNCAN HINES® Creamy Homestyle Vanilla Frosting

½ cup JIF® Creamy Peanut Butter

15 miniature peanut butter cup candies, wrappers removed, cut in half vertically

1. Preheat oven to 350°F. Place 30 (2½-inch) paper liners in muffin cups.

2. Prepare, bake and cool cupcakes following package directions for basic recipe.

3. Combine Vanilla frosting and peanut butter in medium bowl. Stir until smooth.

4. Frost one cupcake. Decorate with peanut butter cup candy, cut-side down. Repeat with remaining cupcakes.   *Makes 30 servings*

....

Cook's Notes:

You may substitute DUNCAN HINES® Moist Deluxe® Devil's Food, Dark Chocolate Fudge or Butter Recipe Fudge Cake Mix flavors for Swiss Chocolate Cake Mix.

....

EASY EASEL
RECIPES

CHOCOLATE CARAMEL PECAN BARS

2 cups butter, softened, divided
½ cup granulated sugar, divided
1 egg
2¾ cups all-purpose flour
⅔ cup packed light brown sugar
¼ cup light corn syrup
2½ cups coarsely chopped pecans
1 cup semisweet chocolate chips

1. Preheat oven to 375°F. Grease 15×10-inch jelly-roll pan; set aside.

2. Beat 1 cup butter and granulated sugar in large bowl with electric mixer at medium speed until light and fluffy. Beat in egg. Add flour. Beat at low speed until just blended. Spread dough into prepared pan. Bake 20 minutes or until light golden brown.

3. Meanwhile, prepare topping. Combine remaining 1 cup butter, brown sugar and corn syrup in medium saucepan. Bring to a boil over medium heat stirring frequently. Boil 2 minutes without stirring. Quickly stir in pecans; spread over base. Bake 20 minutes or until dark golden brown and bubbling.

4. Immediately sprinkle chocolate chips evenly over hot caramel. Gently press chips into caramel topping with spatula. Loosen caramel from edges of pan with spatula or knife. Remove pan to wire rack; cool completely. Cut into 3×1½-inch bars.

Makes 40 bars

EASY EASEL RECIPES

DEEP DARK CHOCOLATE CAKE

2 cups sugar
1¾ cups all-purpose flour
¾ cup HERSHEY'S Cocoa or HERSHEY'S Dutch Processed Cocoa
1½ teaspoons baking powder
1½ teaspoons baking soda
1 teaspoon salt
2 eggs
1 cup milk
½ cup vegetable oil
2 teaspoons vanilla extract
1 cup boiling water
One-Bowl Buttercream Frosting (recipe follows)

Heat oven to 350°F. Grease and flour two 9-inch round baking pans. In large mixer bowl, stir together sugar, flour, cocoa, baking powder, baking soda and salt. Add eggs, milk, oil and vanilla; beat on medium speed of electric mixer 2 minutes. Stir in water. (Batter will be thin.) Pour batter evenly into prepared pans. Bake 30 to 35 minutes or until wooden pick inserted in center comes out clean. Cool 10 minutes; remove from pans to wire racks. Cool completely. Prepare One-Bowl Buttercream Frosting; spread between layers and over top and sides of cake. *Makes 8 to 10 servings*

One-Bowl Buttercream Frosting

6 tablespoons butter or margarine, softened
2⅔ cups powdered sugar
½ cup HERSHEY'S Cocoa
⅓ cup milk
1 teaspoon vanilla extract

In small mixer bowl, beat butter. Blend in powdered sugar and cocoa alternately with milk, beating well after each addition until smooth and of spreading consistency. Blend in vanilla. Add additional milk, if needed.

DOUBLE-DECKER CEREAL TREATS

1⅔ cups (10-ounce package) REESE'S® Peanut Butter Chips
2 tablespoons vegetable oil
2 teaspoons vanilla extract, divided
2 cups (12-ounce package) HERSHEY'S® Semi-Sweet Chocolate Chips
2 cups light corn syrup
1⅓ cups packed light brown sugar
12 cups crisp rice cereal, divided

Line 15½×10½×1-inch jelly-roll pan with foil, extending foil over edges of pan.

In large bowl, place peanut butter chips, oil and 1 teaspoon vanilla. In second large bowl, place chocolate chips and remaining 1 teaspoon vanilla.

In large saucepan, stir together corn syrup and brown sugar; cook over

medium heat, stirring constantly, until mixture comes to full rolling boil. Remove from heat. Immediately pour half of hot mixture into each reserved bowl; stir each mixture until chips are melted and mixture is smooth. Immediately stir 6 cups rice cereal into each of the two mixtures.

Spread peanut butter mixture into prepared pan; spread chocolate mixture over top of peanut butter layer. Cool completely. Use foil to lift treats out of pan; peel off foil. Cut treats into bars. Store in tightly covered container in cool, dry place.

Makes about 6 dozen pieces

CHOCOLATE-CHOCOLATE CAKE

1 package (8 ounces) PHILADELPHIA BRAND® Cream Cheese, softened
1 cup BREAKSTONE'S® or KNUDSEN® Sour Cream
½ cup coffee-flavored liqueur or water
2 eggs
1 package (2-layer size) chocolate cake mix
1 package (4-serving size) JELL-O® Chocolate Flavor Instant Pudding and Pie Filling
1 cup BAKER'S® Semi-Sweet Real Chocolate Chips

MIX cream cheese, sour cream, liqueur and eggs with electric mixer on medium speed until well blended. Add cake mix and pudding mix; beat until well blended. Fold in chips. (Batter will be stiff.)

POUR into greased and floured 12-cup fluted tube pan.

BAKE at 325°F for 1 hour to 1 hour and 5 minutes or until toothpick inserted near center comes out clean. Cool 5 minutes. Remove from pan. Cool completely on wire rack. Sprinkle with powdered sugar before serving. Garnish, if desired.

Makes 10 to 12 servings

EASY EASEL RECIPES

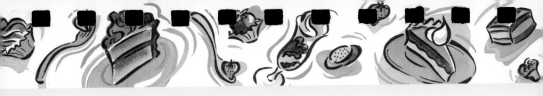

COLORFUL CARAMEL BITES

1 cup plus 6 tablespoons all-purpose flour, divided

1 cup quick-cooking or old-fashioned oats, uncooked

¾ cup firmly packed light brown sugar

½ teaspoon baking soda

¼ teaspoon salt

¾ cup (1½ sticks) butter or margarine, melted

1¾ cups "M&M's"® Semi-Sweet Chocolate Mini Baking Bits, divided

1½ cups chopped pecans, divided

1 jar (12 ounces) caramel ice cream topping

Preheat oven to 350°F.

Combine 1 cup flour, oats, sugar, baking soda and salt; blend in melted butter to form crumbly mixture. Press half the crumb mixture onto bottom of 9×9×2-inch baking pan; bake 10 minutes. Sprinkle with 1 cup baking bits and 1 cup nuts. Blend remaining 6 tablespoons flour with caramel topping; pour over top. Combine remaining crumb mixture, remaining ¾ cup baking bits and remaining ½ cup nuts; sprinkle over caramel layer. Bake 20 to 25 minutes or until golden brown. Cool completely. Cut into squares.

Makes 36 bars

SIMPLE BOSTON CREAM PIES

1 package DUNCAN HINES® Moist
  Deluxe® Yellow Cake Mix
4 containers (3½ ounces each)
  ready-to-eat vanilla pudding
1 container DUNCAN HINES® Creamy
  Homestyle Chocolate Frosting

1. Preheat oven to 350°F. Grease and flour two 8- or 9-inch round pans.

2. Prepare, bake and cool cake following package directions for basic recipe.

3. To assemble, place each cake layer on serving plate. Split layers in half horizontally. Spread contents of 2 containers of vanilla pudding on bottom layer of one cake. Place top layer on filling. Repeat for second cake layer. Remove lid and foil top of

Chocolate frosting container. Heat in microwave oven at HIGH (100% power) 25 to 30 seconds. Stir. (Mixture should be thin.) Spread half the chocolate glaze over top of each cake. Refrigerate until ready to serve.

Makes 12 to 16 servings

Cook's Notes:

For a richer flavor, substitute DUNCAN HINES® Moist Deluxe® Butter Recipe Golden Cake Mix in place of Yellow Cake Mix.

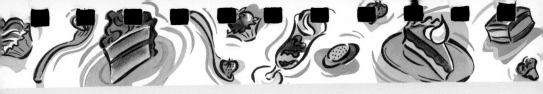

CHOCOLATE PECAN POPCORN BARS

3 quarts popped corn
2 cups pecan halves or coarsely chopped pecans
2 cups (12 ounces) semisweet chocolate chips
¾ cup sugar
¾ cup KARO® Light or Dark Corn Syrup
2 tablespoons MAZOLA® Margarine

1. Preheat oven to 300°F. In large roasting pan combine popped corn and pecans.

2. In medium saucepan combine chocolate chips, sugar, corn syrup and margarine. Stirring occasionally, bring to boil over medium-high heat; boil 1 minute. Pour over popcorn mixture; toss to coat well.

3. Bake 30 minutes, stirring twice.

4. Spoon into 13×9-inch baking pan. Press warm mixture firmly and evenly into pan. Cool 5 minutes. Invert onto cutting board. Cut into bars.   *Makes about 30 bars*

Cook's Notes:

Corn syrup is a thick, sweet syrup made from processing corn starch. Both dark and light corn syrups are available; dark syrup has a stronger flavor and darker color than light syrup.

EASY EASEL® RECIPES

Chocoholic Cakes

Chocolate Cherry Torte (page 75)